giada's family dinners

giada's family dinners
GIADA DE LAURENTIIS

photographs by victoria pearson

Clarkson Potter/Publishers
New York

ALSO BY GIADA DE LAURENTIIS

Everyday Italian

All rights reserved. Published in the United States by
Clarkson Potter/Publishers, an imprint of the Crown Publishing Group,
a division of Random House, Inc., New York.
www.crownpublishing.com
www.clarksonpotter.com

Clarkson N. Potter is a trademark and Potter and colophon are
registered trademarks of Random House, Inc.

Library of Congress Cataloging-in-Publication Data
De Laurentiis, Giada.
Giada's family dinners / Giada De Laurentiis; photographs
by Victoria Pearson.—1st ed.
Includes index.   1. Cookery, Italian.   2. Family—Nutrition.
3. Quick and easy cookery.   I. Title: Family dinners.   II. Title.
TX723.D326   2006
641.5945—dc22   2005021630

ISBN-13: 978-0-307-23827-6
ISBN-10: 0-307-23827-X

Printed in the United States of America

Design by Jan Derevjanik

8   9   10

**To my family,
for giving me the courage, spirit,
knowledge, and passion to do what I love!**

introduction

Welcome to my family, where life is shared in the kitchen and around the table over recipes that have been handed down through generations. Where we stay close and take time to be with one another. Where we define ourselves by the food we eat and the stories we tell, as we pass plates and bowls around the table.

This is the kind of unpretentious, authentic, down-home Italian cooking that my family loves. It represents an unbroken line from my grandfather (who gave me my love of food), to Italy (where I was born), to my extended family's life today in America. There is a lot of tradition in this book, and a lot of love.

Some of these recipes are special-occasion dishes in my household, but you shouldn't wait for a special occasion to entertain. A family-style meal is all about sharing. It's not about getting dressed up, or serving food so fancy that people are afraid to stick a fork into it. It's a chance to take a step back from everyday worries and focus on what really matters.

This is accessible and uncomplicated home-style cooking. With many of the recipes, it doesn't matter if you're cooking for four or fifteen; changing the quantities is easy. The recipes are flexible and nearly foolproof, so you don't have to worry about making everything perfect.

In my opinion—one colored by my family's rich culinary traditions—anytime you invite someone into your home and cook for them, you are making them part of your family. So don't worry about finishing all your preparations before the guests arrive. Invite everyone into the kitchen to help make the meal you'll share together. Personally, I am honored when someone asks me to help in the kitchen. That's when I know they're really letting me into their life.

So that's why I've chosen to gather my favorite family-style recipes, those that are a bit more casual both to make and to serve. It's fun food, nothing too fancy, but it's all deeply satisfying. After all, you're also inviting me into your home by making these dishes; I want you to be proud when you serve them.

Traditions help us understand who we are and where we come from. Sharing a meal helps define who we are as a family. Hopefully in this book you'll find heaping portions of tradition and culture, of good food and family togetherness. And perhaps it will inspire you to create new traditions of your own.

SOUPS
and
SANDWICHES

Soups and sandwiches are both simple and

economical. In Italy they are traditionally created from whatever is on hand, so they're a great way to use up leftovers. Soups are easy: most of them start with the traditional *sofrito* of onions, carrots, celery, and garlic. You sauté them together, add the rest of your ingredients and some liquid, then walk away.

Here in America (and in Italy, too) soup is thought of primarily as lunch food, but when I was growing up it was often what we ate at dinnertime—especially on those nights when my mother was too tired to cook something more elaborate. What I love about making soup for dinner is that there are always leftovers for the next day and the flavor only improves overnight.

Sandwiches are considered more of a snack than a meal in Italy, so those you'll find in this chapter are really Italian-American creations. And my recipes are just suggestions; more than almost any other dish, a sandwich leaves room for improvisation. Experiment, and have fun.

BEEF AND LENTIL SOUP

TOMATO SOUP WITH PANCETTA

PASTA E FAGIOLI

WINTER MINESTRONE

ESCAROLE AND BEAN SOUP

ITALIAN WEDDING SOUP

STRACCIATELLA SOUP

TUNA AND ARTICHOKE PANINI

VENETIAN PANINO

VEGETABLE PANINI WITH MOZZARELLA

PROSCIUTTO AND MELON PANINI

OPEN-FACED PLT

ITALIAN MUFFULETTA

beef and lentil soup

Growing up, I ate lots of lentils—in soups, salads, stews—and I still love them. My favorite way to eat them is in a hearty soup. This is a twist on the classic recipe, with big chunks of beef and lots of herbs and vegetables. It's like a meal in a bowl.

2	TABLESPOONS OLIVE OIL
1½	POUNDS BONELESS BEEF CHUCK, CUT INTO 1-INCH CUBES
	SALT AND FRESHLY GROUND BLACK PEPPER
3	LARGE CELERY STALKS, CHOPPED
2	LARGE CARROTS, PEELED AND CHOPPED
1	LARGE ONION, CHOPPED
6	GARLIC CLOVES, CHOPPED
1½	TEASPOONS CHOPPED FRESH ROSEMARY
1½	TEASPOONS DRIED OREGANO
6	(14-OUNCE) CANS (OR MORE) LOW-SODIUM BEEF BROTH
1	(28-OUNCE) CAN DICED TOMATOES IN JUICE
2	CUPS (ABOUT 11 OUNCES) LENTILS, RINSED
⅓	CUP CHOPPED FRESH FLAT-LEAF PARSLEY

Heat the oil in a large, heavy pot over medium-high heat. Season the beef with salt and pepper. Working in two batches, add the beef to the pot and cook until browned all over, about 8 minutes. Use a slotted spoon to transfer the beef to a bowl.

Add the celery, carrots, onion, garlic, rosemary, and oregano to the pot. Sauté until the onions are translucent, about 8 minutes. Return the beef and any accumulated juices from the bowl to the pot. Add the broth and the tomatoes with their juice. Bring the soup to a boil, then reduce the heat to medium-low. Cover and simmer, stirring occasionally, until the meat is just tender, about 1 hour. Add the lentils. Cover and continue simmering until the lentils are tender, about 40 minutes. Stir in the parsley. Season the soup to taste with salt and pepper.

tomato soup with pancetta

This recipe is made almost entirely from pantry items—all things you should have on hand. It's incredibly quick to prepare and cook. The rye bread and pancetta give the soup its hearty flavor; the mascarpone adds a bit of richness and smoothes it all out.

- 1 TABLESPOON OLIVE OIL
- 3 OUNCES PANCETTA, CHOPPED
- 1 MEDIUM ONION, CHOPPED
- 3 ($\frac{3}{4}$-INCH-THICK) SLICES RUSTIC RYE BREAD (EACH ABOUT $5\frac{3}{4} \times 3\frac{3}{4}$ INCHES), CUBED
- 6 CUPS REDUCED-SODIUM CHICKEN BROTH
- 1 (28-OUNCE) CAN DICED TOMATOES IN JUICE
- $\frac{1}{4}$ CUP COARSELY CHOPPED FRESH BASIL
- $\frac{1}{2}$ TEASPOON DRIED OREGANO
- $\frac{1}{4}$ TEASPOON CRUSHED DRIED RED PEPPER FLAKES
  SALT AND FRESHLY GROUND BLACK PEPPER
- $\frac{1}{4}$ CUP MASCARPONE CHEESE
- $\frac{1}{4}$ CUP SOUR CREAM

Heat the oil in a large, heavy pot over a medium flame. Add the pancetta and sauté until crisp and golden, about 5 minutes. Add the onion and sauté until tender, about 3 minutes. Add the bread cubes and toss to coat with the pan drippings. Sauté until the bread cubes are golden, about 5 minutes. Add the broth, tomatoes, basil, oregano, and red pepper flakes. Bring the soup to a boil, then reduce the heat to medium-low. Simmer uncovered until the flavors blend, about 10 minutes. Season the soup to taste with salt and pepper.

In a small bowl, stir together the mascarpone and sour cream until blended. Ladle the soup into bowls. Spoon a dollop of the mascarpone mixture onto each serving and serve.

pasta e fagioli

This is the classic Italian comfort-food soup, here livened up with fresh herbs. If you don't have any thyme or rosemary, feel free to substitute dried. Any small shaped pasta will do.

- 4 **SPRIGS OF FRESH THYME**
- 1 **LARGE FRESH ROSEMARY SPRIG**
- 1 **BAY LEAF**
- 1 **TABLESPOON OLIVE OIL**
- 1 **TABLESPOON UNSALTED BUTTER**
- 1 **CUP CHOPPED ONION**
- 3 **OUNCES PANCETTA OR BACON, CHOPPED**
- 2 **GARLIC CLOVES, MINCED**
- 5¾ **CUPS REDUCED-SODIUM CHICKEN BROTH**
- 2 **(14½-OUNCE) CANS RED KIDNEY BEANS, RINSED AND DRAINED**
- ¾ **CUP ELBOW MACARONI**
  FRESHLY GROUND BLACK PEPPER
- ⅓ **CUP FRESHLY GRATED PARMESAN CHEESE**
- 1 **TABLESPOON EXTRA-VIRGIN OLIVE OIL**

Wrap the thyme, rosemary, and bay leaf in a piece of cheesecloth and tie it with kitchen twine. Heat the olive oil and butter in a large, heavy saucepan over a medium flame. Add the onion, pancetta, and garlic and sauté until the onion is tender, about 3 minutes. Add the broth, beans, and sachet of herbs. Cover and bring to a boil over high heat, then decrease the heat to medium and simmer until the vegetables are very tender, about 10 minutes. Discard the sachet.

In a blender, purée 1 cup of the bean mixture until smooth, then return the purée to the saucepan. Cover and return the soup to a boil over high heat. Add the macaroni, cover, and boil, stirring occasionally, until the macaroni is tender but still firm to the bite, about 8 minutes. Season the soup with pepper.

Ladle the soup into bowls. Sprinkle with Parmesan cheese and drizzle with extra-virgin olive oil.

winter minestrone

4 TO 6 SERVINGS

Never throw away a Parmesan cheese rind; it is the secret to this soup. As the soup simmers, the cheese rind slowly releases its salty, buttery goodness and leaves the soup silky and yummy. Make a double batch and eat it for days with crusty bread.

- 2 **TABLESPOONS OLIVE OIL**
- 1 **ONION, CHOPPED**
- 2 **CARROTS, PEELED AND CHOPPED**
- 2 **CELERY STALKS, CHOPPED**
- 3 **OUNCES THINLY SLICED PANCETTA, COARSELY CHOPPED**
- 2 **GARLIC CLOVES, MINCED**
- 1 **POUND SWISS CHARD, STEMS TRIMMED, LEAVES COARSELY CHOPPED**
- 1 **RUSSET POTATO, PEELED AND CUBED**
- 1 **(14½-OUNCE) CAN DICED TOMATOES IN JUICE**
- 2 **FRESH ROSEMARY SPRIGS**
- 1 **(15-OUNCE) CAN CANNELLINI BEANS, DRAINED AND RINSED**
- 2 **(14-OUNCE) CANS LOW-SODIUM BEEF BROTH**
  1-OUNCE PIECE OF PARMESAN CHEESE RIND
- 2 **TABLESPOONS CHOPPED FRESH FLAT-LEAF PARSLEY**
  SALT AND FRESHLY GROUND PEPPER

Heat the oil in a large, heavy pot over medium heat. Add the onion, carrots, celery, pancetta, and garlic. Sauté until the onion is translucent, about 10 minutes. Add the Swiss chard and potato; sauté for 2 minutes. Add the tomatoes with juice and the rosemary sprigs. Simmer until the chard is wilted and the tomatoes break down, about 10 minutes.

Meanwhile, in a food processor, combine ¾ cup of the beans with ¼ cup of the broth, and blend until almost smooth. Add the puréed bean mixture, remaining broth, and Parmesan rind to the vegetable mixture. Simmer until the potato pieces are tender, stirring occasionally, about 15 minutes. Stir in the remaining beans and the parsley. Simmer until the beans are heated through and the soup is thick, about 2 minutes. Season with salt and pepper to taste. Discard the rosemary stems (the needles will have fallen off).

Ladle the soup into bowls and serve.

escarole and bean soup

6 SERVINGS

This is probably the fastest soup you'll ever throw together. I sometimes add sausage to make it a little heartier.

- 2 TABLESPOONS OLIVE OIL
- 2 GARLIC CLOVES, CHOPPED
- 1 POUND ESCAROLE, CHOPPED
- 4 CUPS REDUCED-SODIUM CHICKEN BROTH
- 1 (15-OUNCE) CAN CANNELLINI BEANS, DRAINED AND RINSED
- 1-OUNCE CHUNK OF PARMESAN CHEESE
- SALT AND FRESHLY GROUND BLACK PEPPER
- 6 TEASPOONS EXTRA-VIRGIN OLIVE OIL
- CRUSTY BREAD, FOR SERVING

Heat the olive oil in a large, heavy pot over medium heat. Add the garlic and sauté until fragrant, about 30 seconds. Add the escarole and sauté until wilted, about 3 minutes. Add the chicken broth, beans, and chunk of Parmesan cheese. Simmer until the beans are heated through, about 5 minutes. Season with salt and pepper to taste.

Ladle the soup into 6 bowls. Drizzle 1 teaspoon extra-virgin olive oil over each portion. Serve with crusty bread.

italian wedding soup

Traditionally this soup was served at Italian weddings, but we make it any time. Kids particularly seem to love this soup. My mother always made very small meatballs and I like it best that way, though I have seen this served with just a few, larger meatballs as well.

meatballs

- 1 SMALL ONION, GRATED
- ¼ CUP CHOPPED FRESH FLAT-LEAF PARSLEY
- 1 LARGE EGG
- 4 GARLIC CLOVES, MINCED
- 1 TEASPOON SALT
- ¼ TEASPOON FRESHLY GROUND BLACK PEPPER
- ½ CUP FRESHLY GRATED PARMESAN CHEESE
- ¼ CUP PLAIN DRIED BREAD CRUMBS
- 8 OUNCES LEAN GROUND BEEF (15% FAT)
- 8 OUNCES GROUND PORK

soup

- 10 CUPS REDUCED-SODIUM CHICKEN BROTH
- 1 POUND ESCAROLE, COARSELY CHOPPED
- 2 LARGE EGGS
- ⅔ CUP FRESHLY GRATED PARMESAN CHEESE
- SALT AND FRESHLY GROUND BLACK PEPPER

to make the meatballs

In a large bowl, stir together the onion, parsley, egg, garlic, salt, and pepper. Stir in the cheese and bread crumbs. Using your hands, mix in the ground beef and pork. Shape the mixture into 1-inch meatballs, making approximately 75 balls. Place on a baking sheet.

to make the soup

Bring the broth to a boil in a large pot over medium-high heat. Add the meatballs and escarole and simmer until the meatballs are cooked through and the escarole is tender, about 10 minutes. In a medium bowl, whisk together the eggs and cheese. Add the egg mixture to the soup slowly, stirring with a fork to form thin strands of egg, about 1 minute. Season the soup to taste with salt and pepper.

Ladle the soup into bowls and serve.

tuna and artichoke panini

Here's where having a well-stocked pantry comes to the rescue—almost everything in this gutsy Mediterranean sandwich comes right off the shelf. The filling is equally good served over a green salad or even tossed with some hot or cool cooked pasta.

¾ **CUP PITTED KALAMATA OLIVES**

2 **TABLESPOONS OLIVE OIL**

2 **GARLIC CLOVES**

1 **TEASPOON LEMON ZEST**

¼ **CUP MAYONNAISE**

2 **(6-OUNCE) CANS OIL-PACKED TUNA, DRAINED**

1 **(12-OUNCE) JAR MARINATED ARTICHOKES, DRAINED AND COARSELY CHOPPED**

1 **TEASPOON FRESH LEMON JUICE**

½ **TEASPOON FRESHLY GROUND BLACK PEPPER**

1 **(1-POUND) LOAF CIABATTA OR OTHER COUNTRY-STYLE WHITE BREAD, HALVED HORIZONTALLY**

1 **TOMATO, DICED**

In a food processor, combine the olives, oil, garlic, and zest, and purée until smooth and spreadable. Blend in the mayonnaise. In a medium bowl, toss the tuna, artichokes, lemon juice, and pepper, keeping the tuna in small chunks.

Hollow out the bottom and top halves of the bread. Spread the olive purée over both cut sides of the bread. Spoon the tuna-and-artichoke mixture onto the bottom half of the bread. Sprinkle the tomatoes over. Cover with the bread top. Press the sandwich lightly with your palm, then cut the sandwich crosswise into 6 pieces.

stracciatella soup

4 TO 6 SERVINGS

This is the basic *stracciatella* soup that my mother made for me as a child. The name means "little rags," which refers to the strands of egg, but you could add other ingredients to jazz it up, like spinach leaves, chicken, tofu. . . . This simple version tastes like home to me. However you like it, it's light but very satisfying.

- 6 CUPS REDUCED-SODIUM CHICKEN BROTH
- 2 LARGE EGGS
- 2 TABLESPOONS FRESHLY GRATED PARMESAN CHEESE
- 2 TABLESPOONS CHOPPED FRESH FLAT-LEAF PARSLEY
- 2 TABLESPOONS CHOPPED FRESH BASIL
- 1 CUP LIGHTLY PACKED SPINACH LEAVES, CUT IN THIN STRIPS
   SALT AND FRESHLY GROUND BLACK PEPPER

Bring the broth to a boil in a large saucepan over medium-high heat. In a bowl, whisk the eggs, cheese, parsley, and basil to blend. Reduce the heat to medium-low. Stir the broth in a circular motion. Gradually drizzle the egg mixture into the moving broth, stirring gently with a fork to form thin strands of egg, about 1 minute. Stir in the spinach, then season the soup to taste with salt and pepper.

Ladle the soup into bowls and serve.

venetian panino

I had a very similar sandwich at Harry's Bar and Grill in Venice. I've lightened it up by substituting turkey for the ham, but the real star is the cheese spread—it *makes* the sandwich!

- 1 **GARLIC CLOVE**
- 8 **OUNCES GRUYÈRE CHEESE, SHREDDED**
- 2 **TABLESPOONS UNSALTED BUTTER, AT ROOM TEMPERATURE**
- 2 **TABLESPOONS DIJON MUSTARD**
- 12 **OUNCES SLICED TURKEY**
- 12 **SLICES WHEAT OR SOURDOUGH BREAD**
- 6 **TABLESPOONS OLIVE OIL**

Finely chop the garlic in a food processor. Add the cheese, butter, and mustard. Blend until the mixture is thick, smooth, and spreadable.

Spread the cheese mixture over one side of each bread slice. Arrange the turkey slices over the cheese mixture on 6 of the slices. Top the sandwiches with the remaining bread slices, cheese side down, pressing gently to adhere. Trim the crusts from the sandwiches and cut in half on the diagonal.

Heat 3 tablespoons of oil in a large, heavy griddle or skillet over medium-low heat. Cook half of the sandwiches until golden brown and heated through, about 4 minutes per side. Transfer to a serving platter and tent with foil to keep them warm. Repeat with the remaining 3 tablespoons of oil and sandwiches. Serve immediately.

vegetable panini with mozzarella

The key to this hefty sandwich is the fresh mozzarella because its sweet, creamy flavor and texture cannot be matched by the rubbery supermarket kind. I like mine with a little bit of basil pesto, but it's not critical; there's plenty of flavor in the filling either way. This is especially nice for picnics, or serve smaller portions, instead of rolls and a salad, alongside a grilled steak.

1 EGGPLANT, CUT CROSSWISE INTO ½-INCH-THICK SLICES

2 ZUCCHINI, CUT LENGTHWISE INTO ¼-INCH-THICK SLICES

1 SMALL RED ONION, CUT INTO ½-INCH-THICK SLICES

¼ CUP OLIVE OIL

   SALT AND FRESHLY GROUND BLACK PEPPER

½ CUP BASIL PESTO (PAGE 55)

2 BAGUETTES (EACH ABOUT 2 FEET LONG), SPLIT LENGTHWISE

8 OUNCES FRESH WATER-PACKED MOZZARELLA, DRAINED AND SLICED

2 TOMATOES, SLICED

8 LARGE BASIL LEAVES

½ CUP ROASTED BELL PEPPERS, A MIXTURE OF YELLOW AND RED

Heat a grill pan over medium-high heat. Brush the eggplant, zucchini, and onion slices with the oil, then sprinkle with salt and pepper. Working in batches, grill the eggplant, zucchini, and onion until they are tender and grill marks appear, about 4 minutes per side. Cool completely.

Spread the pesto over the cut sides of the baguettes. Arrange the mozzarella over the bottom halves of the baguettes. Top with the tomatoes and sprinkle with salt and pepper. Arrange the grilled eggplant, zucchini, onion, basil leaves, and bell peppers over the tomatoes. Fold the baguettes together, then cut each sandwich crosswise into 3 equal pieces and serve. (The sandwiches can be made 4 hours ahead. Wrap well with plastic wrap and refrigerate.)

**Far left, Prosciutto and Melon Panini;
near left, Vegetable Panini with Mozzarella**

prosciutto and melon panini

MAKES 4 SANDWICHES

Melon with prosciutto is no doubt one of the most popular antipasti. With the addition of silky Brie cheese and yeasty focaccia, this classic flavor combo becomes an outstanding sandwich. Cut each into four squares for a great cocktail bite.

NONSTICK OLIVE OIL COOKING SPRAY

4 (4 × 2-INCH-THICK) SQUARES OF FOCACCIA

8 OUNCES BRIE CHEESE, CUT INTO THIN SLICES

8 PAPER-THIN SLICES PROSCIUTTO

2 CUPS LIGHTLY PACKED ARUGULA

8 THIN SLICES CANTALOUPE

Spray a panini grill or ridged grill pan with nonstick spray. Preheat the panini grill for medium heat according to the manufacturer's instructions, or preheat the grill pan over medium heat. Halve each focaccia square horizontally and arrange half of the cheese over the bottom halves. Arrange the prosciutto, arugula, then the cantaloupe on top of the cheese. Cover with the remaining cheese, then with the focaccia tops.

Working in batches if necessary, grill the sandwiches until the cheese melts and the bread is crisp and golden, about 6 minutes. Cut the sandwiches in half and serve.

open-faced PLT

This is a more refined take on that all-American classic, the BLT. Prosciutto is a bit less assertive (and less greasy) than the usual bacon, and the lemony mayo and peppery arugula give the sandwich lots of lively flavor.

½ **CUP MAYONNAISE**

1 **TABLESPOON FRESH LEMON JUICE**

1 **TABLESPOON LEMON ZEST**

6 **SLICES WHOLE WHEAT OR SOURDOUGH BREAD**

6 **OUNCES THINLY SLICED PROSCIUTTO**

3 **CUPS ARUGULA**

2 **TOMATOES, SLICED**

1 **TABLESPOON EXTRA-VIRGIN OLIVE OIL**

SALT AND FRESHLY GROUND BLACK PEPPER

In a small bowl, whisk the mayonnaise, lemon juice, and zest to blend. Set the mayonnaise mixture aside.

Toast the bread on a panini grill or griddle until golden brown. Spread the mayonnaise mixture over each slice of toast. Arrange the prosciutto over the toasts, dividing equally. Top with the arugula, then the tomatoes. Drizzle the oil over the sandwiches, then sprinkle with salt and pepper. Cut the sandwiches into 3 equal pieces and serve.

italian muffuletta

A takeoff on the classic Italian hero. The combination of sliced meats is flexible; feel free to substitute or omit any of them. But what makes this sandwich a muffuletta is the olive and red pepper spread, so don't skip it!

- ¼ CUP RED WINE VINEGAR
- 2 GARLIC CLOVES, FINELY CHOPPED
- 1 TEASPOON DRIED OREGANO
- ⅓ CUP OLIVE OIL
- 10 LARGE PITTED GREEN OLIVES, CHOPPED
- ⅓ CUP PITTED KALAMATA OLIVES, CHOPPED
- ¼ CUP CHOPPED ROASTED RED BELL PEPPERS
- SALT AND FRESHLY GROUND BLACK PEPPER
- 1 (1-POUND) ROUND BREAD LOAF (ABOUT 7 INCHES IN DIAMETER)
- 4 OUNCES THINLY SLICED HAM
- 4 OUNCES THINLY SLICED MORTADELLA
- 4 OUNCES THINLY SLICED SALAMI
- 4 OUNCES SLICED PROVOLONE CHEESE
- ½ RED ONION, THINLY SLICED
- 1½ OUNCES ARUGULA LEAVES

In a large bowl, whisk the vinegar, garlic, and oregano to blend. Gradually whisk in the oil. Stir in the green and kalamata olives and roasted peppers. Season the vinaigrette with salt and pepper.

Using a serrated knife, slice off the top inch of the bread loaf. Hollow out the bottom and top halves of the loaf. Spread some of the vinaigrette in the bread bottom. Layer the meats and cheese in the bottom half. Top with the onion, then the arugula. Spread the remaining vinaigrette on the cut side of the bread top, then replace the bread top. (The sandwich can be made a day ahead. Wrap with plastic wrap and refrigerate.)

Cut the sandwich into wedges and serve.

ITALIAN SALADS
and
SIDES

I keep vegetable dishes simple, fresh, and exciting. A lot of people consider vegetables a last-minute dish that is best made right before the meal is served. I don't; the time just before I serve is the busiest, so why add to my workload? I rely on these delicious and versatile recipes that can be made ahead of time, or started in advance and finished in just a few minutes when I'm ready to put everything on the table. That way there's never a worry about overcooked vegetables or soggy salads.

More substantial side dishes, like those with orzo or cannellini beans, can even be made up to two days in advance, and they really pack a lot of flavor.

While the salads shouldn't be dressed until right before you serve them, do get all the components ready in advance so you can just toss and serve.

ROASTED BEET AND ARUGULA SALAD
WITH GOAT CHEESE AND AVOCADO

ITALIAN CAESAR SALAD

ARUGULA AND ORANGE SALAD WITH BASIL VINAIGRETTE

BROCCOLI FLORETS WITH MEYER LEMON OLIVE OIL

MARINATED ZUCCHINI AND SUMMER SQUASH

BUTTERNUT SQUASH GRATIN WITH PESTO

ROASTED EGGPLANT AND TOMATOES

SAUTÉED GREEN BEANS WITH TOMATOES AND BASIL

ROASTED FENNEL WITH PARMESAN

**ORZO WITH GARBANZO BEANS, RED ONION,
BASIL, AND MINT**

CANNELLINI BEANS WITH HERBS AND PROSCIUTTO

STUFFED ARTICHOKES

BRAISED SWISS CHARD

BASIC POLENTA

HERBED CHEESE POLENTA

roasted beet and arugula salad with goat cheese and avocado

I happen to *love* beets, probably because they're sweet. Roasting them gives them a deeper, richer flavor than boiling. It's so simple to toss them in the oven, so when I make them, I make a lot so I can eat them all week long, tossed with a little bit of salt, pepper, and vinegar.

- ¼ **CUP BALSAMIC VINEGAR**
- 3 **TABLESPOONS FINELY CHOPPED SHALLOTS**
- 1 **TABLESPOON HONEY**
- ⅓ **CUP OLIVE OIL**
-   **SALT AND FRESHLY GROUND BLACK PEPPER**
- 6 **MEDIUM BEETS, PEELED, EACH CUT INTO 6 WEDGES**
- 6 **CUPS ARUGULA, STEMS REMOVED**
- ½ **CUP TOASTED WALNUTS, COARSELY CHOPPED (SEE PAGE 221)**
- ¼ **CUP DRIED CRANBERRIES OR DRIED CHERRIES**
- ½ **AVOCADO, PEELED, PITTED, AND CUBED**
- 3 **OUNCES GOAT CHEESE, COARSELY CRUMBLED**

Preheat the oven to 400°F. Place a large piece of foil on a heavy baking sheet.

In a medium bowl, whisk the vinegar, shallots, and honey to blend. Gradually whisk in the oil. Season the vinaigrette to taste with salt and pepper.

In another medium bowl, toss the beets with enough dressing to coat. Place the beet mixture in the center of the foil on the baking sheet. Top with another piece of foil and crimp the edges of the foil to seal tightly. Roast the beets until they are tender when pierced with a fork, about 30 minutes. Uncover the beets and continue roasting until they are slightly caramelized, shaking the pan occasionally, about 25 minutes longer. Set aside to cool completely.

In a large bowl, toss the arugula, walnuts, and cranberries with enough of the remaining vinaigrette to coat. Season the salad to taste with salt and pepper. Mound the salad on 4 plates. Arrange the beets around the salad. Sprinkle with the avocado and goat cheese, and serve.

italian caesar salad

Here's a fun Italian twist on a classic salad. To me, the best part is the polenta croutons!

dressing

3 GARLIC CLOVES

4 ANCHOVY FILLETS, CHOPPED

¼ CUP FRESH LEMON JUICE (FROM 2 LEMONS)

1 TABLESPOON DIJON MUSTARD

½ CUP OLIVE OIL

   SALT AND FRESHLY GROUND BLACK PEPPER

polenta croutons

1 TEASPOON OLIVE OIL

2 CUPS BASIC POLENTA (PAGE 67), HOT

   VEGETABLE OIL, FOR DEEP FRYING

salad

2 LARGE HEADS OF ROMAINE LETTUCE, HALVED LENGTHWISE

½ CUP DRAINED OIL-PACKED SUN-DRIED TOMATOES,
   CUT INTO THIN STRIPS

½ CUP TOASTED PINE NUTS (SEE PAGE 221)

1½ OUNCES SHAVED PARMESAN CHEESE

   SALT AND FRESHLY GROUND BLACK PEPPER

for the dressing

In a food processor, finely chop the garlic and anchovies. Blend in the lemon juice and mustard. With the machine running, gradually blend in the oil. Season the dressing to taste with salt and pepper.

for the polenta croutons

Coat a small baking sheet with the oil. Transfer the hot polenta to the baking sheet, spreading it evenly to form an 8 × 5 × ¾-inch-thick rectangle. Cover and refrigerate until cold and firm, about 2 hours.

(recipe continues)

Cut the polenta into ¾-inch cubes. Pat the polenta cubes dry with paper towels. Add enough vegetable oil to a large, heavy frying pan to come 1 inch up the sides of the pan. Heat the oil over high heat. Working in batches of 10, carefully add the polenta cubes to the oil one at a time and fry until golden brown, stirring to keep the cubes separate, about 2 minutes. Using a slotted spoon, transfer the polenta croutons to a paper towel–lined plate to drain any excess oil.

(The dressing and polenta croutons can be prepared a day ahead up to this point. Cover the dressing and polenta croutons separately and refrigerate. Rewarm the polenta croutons on a baking sheet in a 350°F oven before serving.)

for the salad

Prepare a charcoal or gas grill for high heat or preheat a ridged grill pan over high heat. Grill the lettuce until lightly charred, about 2 minutes per side. Cut the lettuce into bite-size pieces.

In a large bowl, combine the warm grilled lettuce with the sun-dried tomatoes, pine nuts, and Parmesan cheese. Toss the salad with enough dressing to coat and season to taste with salt and pepper. Mound the salad on large plates, scatter the warm polenta croutons over the salad, and serve immediately.

arugula and orange salad
with basil vinaigrette

6 SERVINGS

This is quick and fresh tasting—perfect as a warm-weather starter or side dish. Peppery arugula is a great combo with the sweet-tart orange, but feel free to substitute spinach.

- 3 MEDIUM NAVEL ORANGES
- 2 SHALLOTS, MINCED
- 3 TABLESPOONS BALSAMIC VINEGAR
- ⅓ CUP OLIVE OIL
- ¼ CUP FINELY CHOPPED FRESH BASIL
- 10 CUPS ARUGULA, ENDS TRIMMED
- SALT AND FRESHLY GROUND BLACK PEPPER

Using a sharp knife, cut away all peel and white pith from the oranges. Cut the oranges in half lengthwise, then crosswise into ¼ inch thick slices. Set aside.

In a medium bowl, combine the shallots and vinegar. Gradually whisk in the oil. Stir in the basil.

In a large bowl, toss the arugula and orange slices with enough vinaigrette to coat. Season the salad with salt and pepper to taste and toss again.

broccoli florets
with meyer lemon olive oil

DaVero makes a fabulous Meyer Lemon Olive Oil and I use it on everything. Meyer Lemons are sweeter than regular lemons and a bit minty, too, so they create a fruity, refreshing oil that perks up any recipe.

1½ POUNDS BROCCOLI FLORETS

3 TABLESPOONS MEYER LEMON OLIVE OIL

SALT AND FRESHLY GROUND BLACK PEPPER

Fill a large pot with 2 inches of water. Set a steamer rack in the pot. Cover and bring the water to a boil over high heat. Add the broccoli and steam until the broccoli is crisp-tender, about 7 minutes.

Transfer the broccoli florets to a large bowl and toss with the oil. Season the broccoli to taste with salt and pepper, and serve warm.

note: As an alternative to the Meyer Lemon Olive Oil, use 1 tablespoon fresh lemon juice and 2 tablespoons extra-virgin olive oil. If you have fresh mint, add some, finely chopped.

marinated zucchini and summer squash

I nominate this as the perfect side for a casual summer meal, when the farm stands have heaps of beautiful yellow and green squash. Prepped and cooked entirely in advance, it just gets better as you sip your Bellini.

2 TABLESPOONS FRESH LEMON JUICE

2 TABLESPOONS WHITE WINE VINEGAR

1 TABLESPOON MINCED GARLIC

2 TEASPOONS CHOPPED FRESH THYME

⅓ CUP OLIVE OIL

SALT AND FRESHLY GROUND BLACK PEPPER

1 POUND ZUCCHINI (ABOUT 3 LARGE), TRIMMED AND QUARTERED LENGTHWISE

1 POUND YELLOW CROOKNECK SQUASH (ABOUT 3 LARGE), TRIMMED AND QUARTERED LENGTHWISE

In a large bowl, whisk the lemon juice, vinegar, garlic, and thyme to blend. Gradually whisk in the oil. Season the marinade to taste with salt and pepper. Spoon 3 tablespoons of the marinade into a small bowl. Cover and set aside. Add the zucchini and yellow squash to the remaining marinade in the large bowl and toss to coat. Transfer the mixture to a 13 × 9 × 2-inch glass baking dish. Cover and marinate at room temperature for at least 3 hours or refrigerate up to 1 day.

Prepare the barbecue for medium-high heat. Grill the squash pieces, turning occasionally, until they are crisp-tender and brown, about 8 minutes. Transfer them to a platter. Drizzle the reserved marinade over the squash and serve hot or at room temperature.

butternut squash gratin with pesto

6 SERVINGS

This looks as good as it tastes and is almost ridiculously rich and substantial, making it a wonderful autumn or winter side dish, especially with a roast. And the beauty of this recipe is that it is made entirely in advance. It can cook right along with the main course if you are roasting a leg of lamb or beef rib roast.

2 TABLESPOONS UNSALTED BUTTER, CUT INTO
    ½-INCH PIECES, PLUS MORE FOR BAKING DISH

1 (3-POUND) BUTTERNUT SQUASH, PEELED, SEEDED,
    AND CUT INTO 1-INCH CUBES

SALT AND FRESHLY GROUND BLACK PEPPER

¼ CUP BASIL PESTO (RECIPE FOLLOWS)

½ CUP FRESHLY GRATED PARMESAN CHEESE

Preheat the oven to 350°F. Lightly butter an 8-inch baking dish. Fill a large pot with 2 inches of water. Set a steamer rack in the pot. Cover and bring the water to a boil over high heat. Add the squash and steam over medium heat until the squash is very tender, about 20 minutes. Transfer the squash to a food processor and blend until smooth and creamy. Season the squash to taste with salt and pepper.

Spoon half of the squash evenly into the prepared baking dish. Dollop half of the pesto all over the squash and sprinkle with half of the cheese. Repeat layering with the remaining squash, pesto, and cheese. Using a skewer, swirl the pesto decoratively into the squash. Dot the top with the butter and bake until the gratin is heated through and golden brown around the edges, about 40 minutes.

basil pesto

MAKES 1 CUP

- **2 CUPS PACKED FRESH BASIL LEAVES**
- **¼ CUP TOASTED PINE NUTS (SEE PAGE 221)**
- **1 GARLIC CLOVE**
- **½ TEASPOON SALT, PLUS MORE TO TASTE**
- **¼ TEASPOON FRESHLY GROUND BLACK PEPPER, PLUS MORE TO TASTE**
- **ABOUT ⅔ CUP EXTRA-VIRGIN OLIVE OIL**
- **½ CUP FRESHLY GRATED PARMESAN CHEESE**

In a blender, pulse the basil, pine nuts, garlic, ½ teaspoon of salt, and ¼ teaspoon of pepper until finely chopped. With the blender still running, gradually add enough oil to form a smooth and thick consistency. Transfer the pesto to a medium bowl and stir in the cheese. Season the pesto with more salt and pepper to taste. (The pesto can be made 2 days ahead. Cover and refrigerate.)

roasted eggplant and tomatoes

I love big, smooth purple eggplants, but when I'm looking for a shortcut and don't want to take the time to salt them (which rids them of any bitter flavor), I use the more petite Japanese eggplants—they're the same color but thinner and not bitter. For this dish they make a better presentation, too.

- **4 JAPANESE EGGPLANTS, HALVED LENGTHWISE**
- **4 ROMA TOMATOES, HALVED LENGTHWISE**
- **6 TABLESPOONS OLIVE OIL**
- **SALT AND FRESHLY GROUND BLACK PEPPER**
- **4 TEASPOONS MINCED GARLIC**
- **½ TEASPOON DRIED OREGANO**
- **1 (14½-OUNCE) CAN DICED TOMATOES IN JUICE, DRAINED**
- **⅓ CUP PLAIN DRIED BREAD CRUMBS**

Preheat the oven to 450°F. Line a large, heavy baking sheet with foil. Cut crosshatch marks over the cut surface of the eggplants. Arrange the eggplants and the Roma tomatoes cut side up on the prepared baking sheet. Brush with 2 tablespoons of the oil. Sprinkle with salt and pepper.

In a small bowl, whisk 2 tablespoons of the oil, 2 teaspoons of the garlic, and ¼ teaspoon of the oregano to blend. Stir in the diced tomatoes. Spoon the mixture over the eggplants. Sprinkle the topping with salt and pepper.

In another small bowl, stir the bread crumbs, the remaining 2 tablespoons of oil, 2 teaspoons of garlic, and ¼ teaspoon of oregano to blend. Sprinkle the bread crumb mixture over the Roma tomatoes.

Bake until the vegetables are tender and the bread crumb topping is brown, about 30 minutes.

sautéed green beans with tomatoes and basil

This was a staple side dish in my house during the holidays, but they're good any time of the year when you need something green on the table. Green beans can be pretty boring, so this is a great way to jazz them up—and they look festive, too!

- 1½ **POUNDS FRESH GREEN BEANS, TRIMMED**
- 2 **TABLESPOONS UNSALTED BUTTER**
- 1 **TABLESPOON OLIVE OIL**
- 3 **LARGE SHALLOTS, THINLY SLICED**
- 2 **GARLIC CLOVES, MINCED**
- 1 **(14½-OUNCE) CAN DICED TOMATOES IN JUICE**
- ¼ **CUP DRY WHITE WINE**
- 2 **TABLESPOONS THINLY SLICED FRESH BASIL**
- **SALT AND FRESHLY GROUND BLACK PEPPER**

Cook the green beans in a large pot of boiling water until just crisp-tender, about 3 minutes. Drain the beans, then rinse with cold water. Drain again very well and set the beans aside.

Melt the butter and oil in a heavy large skillet over medium heat. Add the shallots and garlic and sauté until tender, about 2 minutes. Add the tomatoes and their juices and cook until heated through, about 3 minutes. Add the beans and cook until the juices evaporate and the beans are almost tender, stirring often, about 10 minutes. Stir in the wine and basil. Simmer 2 minutes longer. Season with salt and pepper to taste. Transfer to a platter or bowl and serve.

roasted fennel with parmesan

Fennel is one of those vegetables that is underappreciated in the United States. In Italy, on the other hand, its versatility makes it one of the most used vegetables. Raw, it has a licorice flavor and a celerylike texture that is very refreshing, but it's also delicious as a cooked vegetable. The licorice flavor mellows a bit and is a great match for salty Parmesan.

- 4 TABLESPOONS OLIVE OIL, PLUS MORE FOR BAKING DISH
- 4 FENNEL BULBS, CUT HORIZONTALLY INTO
  ⅓-INCH-THICK SLICES, FRONDS RESERVED
- SALT AND FRESHLY GROUND BLACK PEPPER
- ⅓ CUP FRESHLY SHREDDED PARMESAN CHEESE

Preheat the oven to 375°F. Lightly oil a 13 × 9 × 2-inch glass baking dish. Arrange the fennel in the dish. Sprinkle with salt and pepper, then with the Parmesan cheese. Drizzle with the oil. Bake until the fennel is fork-tender and golden brown, about 45 minutes. Chop enough fennel fronds to equal 2 teaspoons, then sprinkle over the roasted fennel and serve.

orzo with garbanzo beans, red onion, basil, and mint

6 SERVINGS

Here's another one of those great serve-at-room-temperature recipes. It's actually meant to sit around. Orzo looks like rice but it's pasta. Feel free to substitute rice if it's what you have on hand.

4 CUPS REDUCED-SODIUM CHICKEN BROTH OR WATER

1½ CUPS ORZO

1 (15-OUNCE) CAN GARBANZO BEANS, DRAINED AND RINSED

1½ CUPS MIXED RED AND YELLOW TEARDROP TOMATOES OR GRAPE TOMATOES, HALVED

¾ CUP FINELY CHOPPED RED ONION

½ CUP CHOPPED FRESH BASIL

¼ CUP CHOPPED FRESH MINT

¾ CUP RED WINE VINAIGRETTE (PAGE 62)

SALT AND FRESHLY GROUND BLACK PEPPER

Bring the broth to a boil in a large, heavy saucepan over high heat. Stir in the orzo. Cover partially and cook, stirring frequently, until the orzo is tender but still firm to the bite, about 7 minutes. Drain the orzo through a strainer. Transfer the orzo to a large, wide bowl and toss until the orzo cools slightly. Set aside to cool completely.

Toss the orzo with the beans, tomatoes, onion, basil, mint, and enough vinaigrette to coat; you may not need all ¾ cup. Season the salad to taste with salt and pepper, and serve at room temperature.

red wine vinaigrette

½ CUP RED WINE VINEGAR

¼ CUP FRESH LEMON JUICE

2 TEASPOONS HONEY

2 TEASPOONS SALT

¾ TEASPOON FRESHLY GROUND BLACK PEPPER

1 CUP EXTRA-VIRGIN OLIVE OIL

Mix the vinegar, lemon juice, honey, salt, and pepper in a blender. With the machine running, gradually blend in the oil. Season the vinaigrette to taste with more salt and pepper, if desired.

lemon vinaigrette

MAKES A SCANT ⅔ CUP

2 TEASPOONS FINELY GRATED LEMON ZEST

¼ CUP FRESH LEMON JUICE

¼ CUP LIGHTLY PACKED FRESH FLAT-LEAF PARSLEY LEAVES

2 GARLIC CLOVES, CHOPPED

½ TEASPOON SALT

¼ TEASPOON FRESHLY GROUND BLACK PEPPER

⅓ CUP EXTRA-VIRGIN OLIVE OIL

Blend the lemon zest and juice, parsley, garlic, salt, and pepper in a blender. With the machine running, gradually blend in the oil. Season the vinaigrette to taste with more salt and pepper.

cannellini beans with herbs and prosciutto

4 TO 6 SERVINGS

Is this a hearty salad or a great side dish? Either way, it's a good accompaniment for nearly anything, with the prosciutto providing the perfect salty kick to the creamy beans. Think of it as the Italian version of baked beans and serve it alongside any grilled meats.

- 3 **TABLESPOONS OLIVE OIL**
- 1 **TABLESPOON MINCED GARLIC**
- 1 **TABLESPOON CHOPPED FRESH SAGE**
- 2 **TEASPOONS CHOPPED FRESH THYME**
- 1 **(14½-OUNCE) CAN DICED TOMATOES IN JUICE**
- 2 **(15-OUNCE) CANS CANNELLINI BEANS, RINSED AND DRAINED**
- 2 **OUNCES PROSCIUTTO, COARSELY CHOPPED**
  SALT AND FRESHLY GROUND BLACK PEPPER
- 3 **CUPS ARUGULA OR MIXED BABY GREENS**

Heat the oil in a large, heavy skillet over medium heat. Add the garlic and sauté until fragrant, about 30 seconds. Stir in the sage and thyme. Add the tomatoes. Increase the heat to medium-high and simmer for 2 minutes. Add the beans. Simmer until the juices evaporate by half, about 5 minutes. Remove from the heat and stir in the prosciutto. Season the beans to taste with salt and pepper.

Arrange the arugula on a platter. Spoon the beans over the greens and serve.

stuffed artichokes

I know these take a little time to make, but when you're entertaining, they are a sure hit. They can be eaten warm or at room temperature, you can make them ahead, and they look fantastic on a buffet table.

1	LEMON, HALVED
2	WHOLE GARLIC CLOVES
3	LARGE ARTICHOKES
¼	CUP FRESH LEMON JUICE (FROM 2 LEMONS)
3	TABLESPOONS CHOPPED FRESH FLAT-LEAF PARSLEY
2	TABLESPOONS CHOPPED FRESH BASIL
2	TABLESPOONS CHOPPED FRESH MINT
2	GARLIC CLOVES, MINCED
1	TEASPOON GRATED LEMON PEEL
½	CUP OLIVE OIL
	SALT AND FRESHLY GROUND BLACK PEPPER
1¼	POUNDS PLUM TOMATOES, SEEDED AND CHOPPED
2	TABLESPOONS DRAINED CAPERS
3	OUNCES ITALIAN BREAD, CRUST TRIMMED, CUT INTO ½-INCH CUBES
6	FRESH FLAT-LEAF PARSLEY SPRIGS

Squeeze the juice from the lemon halves into a large pot of cold water; add the squeezed lemon halves and the whole garlic cloves. With a heavy sharp knife, cut off the top half of each artichoke and discard. Trim off the stems. Bend back the tough outer leaves and snap off where they break naturally, leaving the tender inner leaves. Using a vegetable peeler, trim the outside of the base until no dark green areas remain. Cut the artichokes in half. Using a small sharp knife, cut out the fibrous choke and small purple-tipped leaves. Submerge the artichoke halves in the lemon water. Boil until the artichokes are tender, 30 to 45 minutes depending on their size. Drain the artichoke halves and set aside to cool while you make the dressing and filling, or if you prefer, cool to room temperature.

In a medium bowl, whisk the lemon juice, parsley, basil, mint, minced garlic, and lemon peel to blend. Gradually whisk in the oil. Season the dressing to taste with salt and pepper.

In a large bowl, toss ⅓ cup of the dressing with the tomatoes and capers. Add the bread cubes and toss to combine. Season the tomato mixture to taste with salt and pepper.

Place 1 artichoke half cut side up on each of 6 plates. Drizzle 1 tablespoon of the dressing over and around each artichoke. Spoon the tomato mixture into the center of the artichoke halves, dividing equally. Garnish with the parsley sprigs and serve.

braised swiss chard

Swiss chard is a leafy green that was very popular in my house when I was young. This is the way I grew up eating it. Spinach is a good substitute, but do give chard a try; it's full of vitamins and calcium, holds its color and shape after cooking, and has a slightly bitter, herbaceous flavor I just love. You can also find red-stemmed ruby chard, which is very pretty on the plate.

- ¼ CUP EXTRA-VIRGIN OLIVE OIL
- 2 LARGE RED ONIONS, SLICED
- 4 GARLIC CLOVES, MINCED
- 4 LARGE BUNCHES OF SWISS CHARD, STEMS TRIMMED AND LEAVES COARSELY CHOPPED
- 4 TOMATOES, COARSELY CHOPPED
- ⅔ CUP REDUCED-SODIUM CHICKEN BROTH
- ¼ CUP SOY SAUCE
- ¾ TEASPOON CRUSHED DRIED RED PEPPER FLAKES
  SALT AND FRESHLY GROUND BLACK PEPPER

Heat the oil in a very large pot over medium heat. Add the onions and garlic, and sauté until tender, about 8 minutes. Add a third of the chard and sauté until it begins to wilt, about 2 minutes. Continue adding the chard a handful at a time, sautéing just until it begins to wilt before adding more. Add the tomatoes, broth, soy sauce, and red pepper flakes. Bring the liquid to a simmer over medium-high heat. Continue simmering, stirring often, until the chard is very tender and the tomatoes soften, about 12 minutes. Season the mixture to taste with salt and black pepper. Transfer the chard to a bowl and serve.

basic polenta

6 SERVINGS

ALT

CORNMEAL

S UNSALTED BUTTER

Bring the water to a boil in a large, heavy saucepan. Add the salt. Gradually whisk in the corn-meal. Reduce the heat to low and cook, stirring often, until the mixture thickens and the corn-meal is tender, about 15 minutes. Remove from the heat. Add the butter and stir until melted.

The polenta is now ready to serve or to spread on a baking sheet or pan to cool, then cut into shapes for grilling, croutons, and so on.

herbed cheese polenta

8 TO 10 SERVINGS

This is the Italian version of mashed potatoes—we serve it with every kind of roast or sautéed meat or poultry. Herbs are a great way to make polenta look and taste upscale.

- 9 CUPS WATER
- 1 TABLESPOON SALT
- 2½ CUPS YELLOW CORNMEAL OR POLENTA
- 1½ CUPS FRESHLY GRATED PARMESAN CHEESE
- 1½ CUPS WHOLE MILK
- 10 TABLESPOONS (1¼ STICKS) UNSALTED BUTTER, CUT INTO PIECES
- ⅓ CUP CHOPPED FRESH FLAT-LEAF PARSLEY
- 1 TABLESPOON FINELY CHOPPED FRESH ROSEMARY
- 1 TABLESPOON CHOPPED FRESH THYME
- ¾ TEASPOON FRESHLY GROUND BLACK PEPPER

Bring the water to a boil in a large, heavy pot. Add the salt. Gradually whisk in the cornmeal. Reduce the heat to low and cook, stirring often, until the mixture thickens and the cornmeal is tender, about 15 minutes. Remove from the heat. Add the cheese, milk, butter, herbs, and pepper. Stir until the butter and cheese melt. Transfer the polenta to a bowl and serve.

Everyday
FAMILY ENTRÉES

Broiled salmon, swordfish Milanese, chicken

tetrazzini, rack of lamb . . . do these impressive entrées sound like a lot of work? Guess again. With the recipes in this chapter, you won't spend all day at the stove—and you won't ruin a good cut of meat, either. Filet mignon with sweet and tangy balsamic syrup, veal scaloppine with a bright, creamy saffron sauce, and a whole roast chicken stuffed with citrus fruit are all impressive entrées that, believe it or not, are a lot of fun to create. While all of these can be made for a crowd of six or eight, they're also great choices for a weeknight family meal for four. You can't go wrong with these sophisticated and mouthwatering showpieces.

PEPPERONCINI SHRIMP

BROILED SALMON WITH GARLIC, MUSTARD, AND HERBS

TILAPIA WITH CITRUS BAGNA CAUDA

SWORDFISH MILANESE

SEA BASS WITH BEANS AND RADICCHIO

CHICKEN MARSALA WITH MUSTARD AND MASCARPONE

POLLO FRITO

CHICKEN TETRAZZINI

GARLIC AND CITRUS CHICKEN

CHICKEN VESUVIO

CHICKEN FLORENTINE

FLANK STEAK WITH RED WINE SAUCE

FILET MIGNON WITH BALSAMIC SYRUP

RACK OF LAMB WITH MINT-BASIL PESTO

VEAL SCALOPPINE WITH SAFFRON CREAM SAUCE

PARMESAN-CRUSTED PORK CHOPS

PORK CHOPS ALLA PIZZAIOLA

LASAGNA ROLLS

STUFFED ZUCCHINI AND RED BELL PEPPERS

pepperoncini shrimp

You can use the pepperoncini oil on any fish as well as on the shrimp. This is also a perfect dish to make on the grill; just slide the shrimp onto wooden skewers (soak them in water for twenty minutes first) to make them easier to handle on the grill.

48 **LARGE SHRIMP (ABOUT 2 POUNDS), PEELED AND DEVEINED**

4 **TEASPOONS PEPPERONCINI OIL (RECIPE FOLLOWS)**

SALT AND FRESHLY GROUND BLACK PEPPER

Heat a large skillet over high heat. Toss the shrimp in a large bowl with the pepperoncini oil. Sprinkle with salt and pepper. Sauté the shrimp until just cooked through, about 2 minutes per side. Add the cooked shrimp to the bowl with the pepperoncini oil and toss again to coat. Transfer the shrimp to a platter and serve.

pepperoncini oil

MAKES ½ CUP

⅓ **CUP OLIVE OIL**

¼ **CUP FINELY CHOPPED PEPPERONCINI**

1 **TABLESPOON MINCED GARLIC**

SALT AND FRESHLY GROUND BLACK PEPPER

Heat the oil in a medium, heavy skillet over medium heat. Add the pepperoncini and garlic and sauté until fragrant, about 2 minutes. Season to taste with salt and pepper. Pour the pepperoncini and oil into a heat-proof bowl and cool to room temperature.

broiled salmon with garlic, mustard, and herbs

6 SERVINGS

I love how the tanginess of the mustard cuts through the rich salmon flavor. You must use both types of mustard, though; Dijon gives the topping its bite and the whole-grain helps create a crust. Dinners don't get much easier (or tastier) than this; the entire preparation and cooking take barely ten minutes.

2 GARLIC CLOVES, MINCED

2 TABLESPOONS DIJON MUSTARD

2 TABLESPOONS WHOLE-GRAIN MUSTARD

¾ TEASPOON FINELY CHOPPED FRESH ROSEMARY

¾ TEASPOON FINELY CHOPPED FRESH THYME

1 TABLESPOON DRY WHITE WINE

1 TABLESPOON OLIVE OIL

NONSTICK OLIVE OIL COOKING SPRAY

6 (6- TO 8-OUNCE) SALMON FILLETS

SALT AND FRESHLY GROUND BLACK PEPPER

6 LEMON WEDGES

In a small bowl, mix the garlic, both mustards, rosemary, and thyme. Mix in the wine and oil. Set the mustard sauce aside.

Preheat the broiler. Line a heavy rimmed baking sheet with foil and spray the foil with non-stick spray. Arrange the salmon fillets on the baking sheet and sprinkle them with salt and pepper. Broil for 2 minutes. Spoon the mustard sauce over the fillets. Continue broiling until the fillets are just cooked through and golden brown, about 5 minutes longer.

Transfer the fillets to plates and serve with the lemon wedges.

tilapia with citrus bagna cauda

6 SERVINGS

Bagna cauda literally means "warm bath." It's a warm garlicky sauce that in the Piedmont region of Italy is used for dipping vegetables. I add some orange juice and lemon zest to lighten the flavors and make it perfect for pouring over the flaky tilapia fillets. Use leftovers to brighten the flavor of steamed cauliflower or simple boiled potatoes.

    3 TABLESPOONS UNSALTED BUTTER

    2 TABLESPOONS EXTRA-VIRGIN OLIVE OIL

    3 ANCHOVY FILLETS, MINCED

 1½ TEASPOONS MINCED GARLIC

    2 TABLESPOONS ORANGE JUICE

    1 TABLESPOON THINLY SLICED FRESH BASIL

    1 TEASPOON LEMON ZEST

    1 TEASPOON ORANGE ZEST

       SALT

    2 TEASPOONS OLIVE OIL

    6 (6-OUNCE) SKINLESS TILAPIA FILLETS

       FRESHLY GROUND BLACK PEPPER

Cook the butter and extra-virgin olive oil in a medium, heavy saucepan over medium heat just until the butter is melted, stirring frequently. Add the anchovies and stir until they dissolve, about 2 minutes. Add the garlic and cook just until fragrant, about 30 seconds. Remove from the heat. Stir in the orange juice, basil, and lemon and orange zests. Season the sauce to taste with salt.

The *bagna cauda* sauce can be made 1 day ahead. Cool, then cover and refrigerate. Rewarm before using.

Meanwhile, preheat the oven to 200°F.

Heat the 2 teaspoons of olive oil in a large, heavy skillet over medium-high heat. Sprinkle the fish with salt and pepper. Working in two batches, cook the fish until just opaque in the center, about 3 minutes per side. Transfer the fish to a platter. Cover with foil and keep warm in the oven while cooking the second batch of fish. When all the fish is cooked, drizzle the sauce over and around the fish and serve.

swordfish milanese

When I was a little girl this was one of the only ways my mom was able to get me to eat fish—her version of fish sticks. The panko is the secret to a flaky crust, but if you can't find it (look in the Asian section of your grocery store, next to the sushi supplies), then feel free to substitute store-bought bread crumbs. I like to place a piece of plastic wrap between the mallet or rolling pin and the fish to keep it from falling apart.

1   CUP PANKO (JAPANESE BREAD CRUMBS)

1   LARGE EGG

4   (5-OUNCE) SWORDFISH STEAKS, EACH ABOUT ½ INCH THICK
    SALT AND FRESHLY GROUND BLACK PEPPER

2   TABLESPOONS UNSALTED BUTTER

2   TABLESPOONS LIGHT OLIVE OIL OR CANOLA OIL

2   TABLESPOONS FRESH LEMON JUICE

2   TABLESPOONS EXTRA-VIRGIN OLIVE OIL

3   CUPS LIGHTLY PACKED ARUGULA

1   BUNCH WATERCRESS, STEMMED

Place the panko in a shallow bowl or pie dish. Beat the egg to blend in another pie dish. Using a meat mallet or heavy rolling pin, gently flatten the swordfish steaks to ¼-inch thickness. Sprinkle a swordfish steak with salt and pepper, then dip into the egg, allowing the excess to drip back into the bowl. Dredge the fish in the panko, coating it completely and patting lightly to adhere the crumbs onto the fish. Place the coated fish on a baking sheet and repeat with the remaining fish steaks.

Melt 1 tablespoon of butter with 1 tablespoon of light olive oil in a heavy large frying pan over medium-high heat. Add two crumb-coated swordfish steaks and cook until brown and crisp and just cooked through, about 1½ minutes per side. Transfer to a plate and tent with foil to keep warm. Wipe out the skillet, then repeat with the remaining butter, light oil, and swordfish steaks.

While the last 2 steaks are cooking, whisk the lemon juice and extra-virgin olive oil in a large bowl to blend. Add the arugula and watercress, and toss to coat. Season the salad to taste with salt and pepper.

Transfer the swordfish steaks to plates. Top with the salad and serve.

sea bass with beans and radicchio

This is one of those recipes that truly gets dinner on the table in a flash. When I've been on the road or indulging in heavy lunches and dinners, this dish lightens me up again. But even though it's not a heavy meal, the beans provide lots of satisfaction and you also get a little bit of a bite from the radicchio. You can use any thin, mild-flavored fresh fillets you prefer, or whatever looks best at the seafood counter.

8 **TABLESPOONS OLIVE OIL**

3 **SHALLOTS, THINLY SLICED**

1 **LARGE HEAD OF RADICCHIO, COARSELY CHOPPED**

1 **(15-OUNCE) CAN CANNELLINI BEANS, DRAINED AND RINSED**

⅓ **CUP FISH BROTH**

SALT AND FRESHLY GROUND BLACK PEPPER

6 **(5- TO 6-OUNCE) SEA BASS, RED SNAPPER, OR SOLE FILLETS**

ALL-PURPOSE FLOUR, FOR DREDGING

LEMON VINAIGRETTE (PAGE 62)

Heat 2 tablespoons of oil in a heavy large skillet over medium heat. Add the shallots and sauté until tender, about 2 minutes. Add the radicchio and sauté until wilted, about 5 minutes. Add the beans and broth, and cook until the beans are heated through, stirring often, about 5 minutes. Season the radicchio mixture to taste with salt and pepper.

Meanwhile, heat 3 tablespoons of oil in each of 2 heavy large frying pans over medium-high heat. Sprinkle the fish fillets with salt and pepper. Dredge the fillets in flour to coat completely, shaking off the excess flour. When the oil is hot, place 3 fillets in each pan and fry until they are golden brown and just cooked through, about 3 minutes per side.

Spoon some of the radicchio mixture onto each plate and top with a fish fillet. Drizzle with the vinaigrette and serve.

chicken marsala with mustard and mascarpone

4 TO 6 SERVINGS

Marsala wine is a Sicilian wine similar to port (Portugal) and sherry (Spain). It's used in both savory and sweet dishes—zabaglione may be the best-known example of the latter. This sauce is a wonderful balance of sweet, tangy, and creaminess.

- 1½ **POUNDS BONELESS, SKINLESS CHICKEN BREAST FILLETS**
  SALT AND FRESHLY GROUND BLACK PEPPER
- 2 **TABLESPOONS OLIVE OIL**
- 5 **TABLESPOONS UNSALTED BUTTER**
- ¾ **CUP CHOPPED ONION**
- 1 **POUND CREMINI MUSHROOMS, TRIMMED AND SLICED**
- 2 **TABLESPOONS MINCED GARLIC**
- 1 **CUP DRY MARSALA WINE**
- 1 **CUP (8 OUNCES) MASCARPONE CHEESE**
- 2 **TABLESPOONS DIJON MUSTARD**
- 2 **TABLESPOONS CHOPPED FRESH FLAT-LEAF PARSLEY, PLUS FRESH FLAT-LEAF PARSLEY SPRIGS, FOR GARNISH**
- 12 **OUNCES DRIED FETTUCCINE**

Sprinkle the chicken with salt and pepper. Heat the oil in a large, heavy skillet over high heat. Add the chicken and cook just until brown, about 4 minutes per side. Set aside.

While the chicken cools, melt 2 tablespoons of the butter in the same skillet over medium-high heat, then add the onion and sauté until it is tender, about 2 minutes. Add the mushrooms and garlic and sauté until the mushrooms are tender and the juices evaporate, about 12 minutes. Add the wine and simmer until it is reduced by half, about 4 minutes. Stir in the mascarpone and mustard. Cut the chicken breasts crosswise into ⅓-inch-thick slices. Return the chicken and any accumulated juices to the skillet. Simmer uncovered over medium-low heat until the chicken is just cooked through and the sauce thickens slightly, about 2 minutes. Stir in 1 tablespoon of the parsley and season the sauce to taste with salt and pepper.

Bring a large pot of salted water to a boil. Add the fettuccine and cook, stirring occasionally, until al dente, about 8 minutes. Drain. Toss with the remaining 3 tablespoons of butter and 1 tablespoon of parsley. Season with salt and pepper. Using tongs, mound the fettuccine on plates. Spoon the chicken mixture over, garnish with parsley sprigs, and serve.

pollo frito

4 SERVINGS

Everybody loves fried chicken, and my family and I are no exceptions. The lemon juice is the secret ingredient to the fresh flavor in this crispy dish. In southern Italy lemons are abundant and are used in everything.

¼   CUP FRESH LEMON JUICE (FROM ABOUT 2 LEMONS)

¼   CUP EXTRA-VIRGIN OLIVE OIL

1½ TEASPOONS SALT

1   TEASPOON FRESHLY GROUND BLACK PEPPER

1   (3½-POUND) FRYING CHICKEN, CUT INTO 8 SERVING PIECES

    APPROXIMATELY 2 CUPS OLIVE OIL, FOR FRYING

1   CUP ALL-PURPOSE FLOUR

    LEMON WEDGES

In a large resealable plastic bag, combine the lemon juice, extra-virgin olive oil, salt, and pepper. Add the chicken pieces and seal the bag. Gently shake the bag to ensure the chicken is coated with the marinade. Refrigerate for at least 2 hours and up to 1 day, turning the bag occasionally.

Preheat the oven to 200°F. In a large cast-iron frying pan or other heavy frying pan, add enough oil to come ⅓ inch up the sides of the pan. Heat the oil over medium heat. Meanwhile, drain the marinade from the chicken and pat the chicken dry with paper towels. Dredge half of the chicken pieces in the flour to coat completely; shake off the excess flour. Add the coated chicken to the hot oil and fry until it is golden brown and just cooked through, turning occasionally, about 25 minutes. Using tongs, transfer the chicken to a paper towel–lined plate to drain the excess oil. Then place the fried chicken on a baking sheet and keep it warm in the oven while frying the remaining chicken. Repeat coating and frying the remaining chicken.

Arrange the fried chicken on a warm platter and serve with the lemon wedges.

chicken tetrazzini

If you've had Tetrazzini only out of a box from the freezer case, it's time to give it another try. It's not exactly a light dish, but we all need a little richness once in a while and this delivers it in every bite. It's also a good way to transform leftover cooked chicken, turkey, or seafood such as shrimp or crabmeat into an indulgent treat.

6 TABLESPOONS (¾ STICK) UNSALTED BUTTER

1 TABLESPOON OLIVE OIL

4 BONELESS, SKINLESS CHICKEN BREAST HALVES

2¼ TEASPOONS SALT, PLUS MORE FOR PASTA

1¼ TEASPOONS FRESHLY GROUND BLACK PEPPER

1 POUND WHITE MUSHROOMS, TRIMMED AND SLICED

1 LARGE ONION, FINELY CHOPPED

5 GARLIC CLOVES, MINCED

1 TABLESPOON CHOPPED FRESH THYME

½ CUP DRY WHITE WINE

⅓ CUP ALL-PURPOSE FLOUR

4 CUPS WHOLE MILK

1 CUP REDUCED-SODIUM CHICKEN BROTH

1 CUP HEAVY CREAM

⅛ TEASPOON GROUND NUTMEG

12 OUNCES DRIED LINGUINE

¾ CUP FROZEN PEAS

¼ CUP CHOPPED FRESH FLAT-LEAF PARSLEY

1 CUP FRESHLY GRATED PARMESAN CHEESE

¼ CUP DRIED ITALIAN-STYLE BREAD CRUMBS

Preheat the oven to 450°F. Use 1 tablespoon of the butter to grease a 13 × 9 × 2-inch baking dish. In a large, deep nonstick frying pan, melt 1 tablespoon of the butter and the oil over medium-high heat. Sprinkle the chicken with ½ teaspoon each of salt and pepper. Add the chicken to the hot pan and cook until pale golden and just cooked through, about 5 minutes per side. Transfer the chicken to a plate to cool slightly. Into a large bowl, coarsely shred the chicken into bite-size pieces.

Meanwhile, add the mushrooms to the same frying pan. Sauté over medium-high heat until the liquid from the mushrooms evaporates and the mushrooms become pale golden, about 12 minutes. Add 1 tablespoon of the butter. When it melts, add the onion, garlic, and thyme, and sauté until the onion is translucent, about 8 minutes. Add the wine and simmer until it evaporates, about 2 minutes. Transfer the mushroom mixture to the bowl with the chicken.

Melt the remaining 3 tablespoons of butter in the same pan over medium-low heat. Add the flour and whisk for 2 minutes. Whisk in the milk, broth, cream, nutmeg, remaining 1¾ teaspoons salt, and remaining ¾ teaspoon pepper. Increase the heat to high. Cover the sauce and bring it to a boil, then simmer uncovered, whisking often, until the sauce thickens slightly, about 1 minute.

Bring a large pot of salted water to a boil. Add the linguine and cook, stirring occasionally, until it is tender but still firm to the bite, about 9 minutes. Drain. Add the linguine, sauce, peas, and parsley to the chicken mixture. Toss until the sauce coats the pasta and the mixture is well blended.

Transfer the pasta mixture to the prepared baking dish. In a small bowl, stir the cheese and bread crumbs to blend. Sprinkle the cheese mixture over the casserole. Bake uncovered until golden brown on top and bubbly, about 25 minutes.

garlic and citrus chicken

Cooking a chicken whole guarantees that the meat will be moist every time. But plain roast chicken can be a bit boring. The bright flavors of citrus fruits make a zesty but still light pan sauce that is a wonderful alternative to traditional gravy.

- 1 (5- TO 6-POUND) WHOLE ROASTING CHICKEN, NECK AND GIBLETS DISCARDED
  SALT AND FRESHLY GROUND BLACK PEPPER
- 1 ORANGE, QUARTERED
- 1 LEMON, QUARTERED
- 1 HEAD OF GARLIC, HALVED CROSSWISE
- 2 (14-OUNCE) CANS REDUCED-SODIUM CHICKEN BROTH
- ¼ CUP FROZEN ORANGE JUICE CONCENTRATE, THAWED
- ¼ CUP FRESH LEMON JUICE (FROM ABOUT 2 LEMONS)
- 2 TABLESPOONS OLIVE OIL
- 1 TABLESPOON CHOPPED FRESH OREGANO
- 3 GARLIC CLOVES, CHOPPED

Position the rack in the center of the oven and preheat the oven to 400°F. Pat the chicken dry and sprinkle the cavity with salt and pepper. Stuff the cavity with the orange, lemon, and garlic halves. Using kitchen twine, tie the chicken legs together to help hold the bird's shape. Sprinkle the chicken with salt and pepper.

Place a rack in a large roasting pan. Place the chicken, breast side up, on the rack in the pan. Roast the chicken for 1 hour, basting occasionally and adding some chicken broth to the pan if necessary to prevent the pan drippings from burning. In a medium bowl, whisk the orange juice, lemon juice, oil, oregano, and chopped garlic to blend. Brush some of the juice mixture over the chicken. Continue roasting the chicken, basting occasionally with the juice mixture and adding broth to the pan, until a meat thermometer inserted into the innermost part of the thigh registers 170°F, about 45 minutes longer. Transfer the chicken to a platter. Tent with foil while making the sauce (do not clean the pan).

Place the same roasting pan over medium-low heat. Whisk in any remaining broth and simmer, stirring often, until the sauce is reduced to 1 cup, about 3 minutes. Strain into a 2-cup glass measuring cup and discard the solids. Spoon the fat from the top of the sauce. Serve the chicken with the pan sauce.

chicken vesuvio

One-pot meals don't get much easier or more elegant than this one, with a deeply flavored, herbaceous sauce and tasty artichokes in the mix. When this dish is simmering the steam that rises from the pot looks like the eruption of Mount Vesuvius.

- 3 **TABLESPOONS OLIVE OIL**
- 2 **CHICKEN BREAST HALVES ON THE BONE WITH SKIN, HALVED CROSSWISE**
- 4 **CHICKEN THIGHS**
  SALT AND FRESHLY GROUND BLACK PEPPER
- 1½ **POUNDS SMALL RED-SKINNED POTATOES, HALVED**
- 6 **LARGE GARLIC CLOVES, MINCED**
- ¾ **CUP DRY WHITE WINE**
- ¾ **CUP REDUCED-SODIUM CHICKEN BROTH**
- 1½ **TEASPOONS DRIED OREGANO**
- 1 **TEASPOON DRIED THYME**
- 8 **OUNCES FROZEN ARTICHOKE HEARTS OR 1 CUP FROZEN LIMA BEANS, THAWED**
- 2 **TABLESPOONS UNSALTED BUTTER**

Preheat the oven to 450°F. Heat the oil in a large ovenproof pot over high heat. Sprinkle the chicken with salt and pepper. Working in batches, cook the chicken until golden brown on all sides, about 10 minutes. Transfer the chicken to a bowl. Add the potatoes to the same pot and cook until they are golden brown, stirring occasionally, about 10 minutes. Add the garlic and sauté for 1 minute. Add the wine and stir to scrape up any brown bits on the bottom of the pot. Add the broth, oregano, and thyme. Return the chicken to the pot, stir to combine, and bring to a boil over medium-high heat.

Cover the pot and transfer it to the oven. Bake until the chicken is cooked through, about 20 minutes. Arrange the chicken and potatoes on a platter. Cover loosely with foil to keep warm. Add the artichoke hearts to the sauce in the pot, then cover and simmer over high heat, stirring often, until the artichokes are tender, about 4 minutes. Remove from the heat. Stir in the butter. Pour the sauce over the chicken and potatoes, and serve.

chicken florentine

4 SERVINGS

Dishes made with spinach have long been associated with Florence. I like the texture of frozen spinach, so I always keep a few boxes in my freezer.

- 4 BONELESS, SKINLESS CHICKEN BREAST HALVES
- SALT AND FRESHLY GROUND BLACK PEPPER
- ALL-PURPOSE FLOUR, FOR DREDGING
- 6 TABLESPOONS (¾ STICK) UNSALTED BUTTER
- 2 TABLESPOONS FINELY CHOPPED SHALLOTS
- 1 TABLESPOON MINCED GARLIC
- 1½ CUPS DRY WHITE WINE
- 1 CUP HEAVY CREAM
- 1 TABLESPOON CHOPPED FRESH FLAT-LEAF PARSLEY
- 2 (10-OUNCE) BOXES FROZEN CUT-LEAF SPINACH, THAWED AND DRAINED

Sprinkle the chicken with salt and pepper. Dredge the chicken in flour to coat lightly; shake off any excess flour. Melt 2 tablespoons of the butter in a large, heavy skillet over medium heat. Add the chicken and cook until brown and just cooked through, about 5 minutes per side. Transfer the chicken to a plate and tent with foil to keep it warm.

Melt 2 tablespoons of the butter in the same skillet over medium heat. Add the shallots and garlic, and sauté until the shallots are translucent, stirring to scrape up any browned bits on the bottom of the skillet, about 1 minute. Add the wine. Increase the heat to medium-high and boil until the liquid is reduced by half, about 3 minutes. Add the cream and boil until the sauce reduces by half again, stirring often, about 3 minutes. Stir in the parsley and season the sauce to taste with salt and pepper. Add the chicken and any accumulated juices to the sauce, and turn the chicken to coat in the sauce.

Meanwhile, melt the remaining 2 tablespoons of butter in another large skillet over medium heat. Add the spinach and sauté until heated through, then season to taste with salt and pepper. Arrange the spinach on a platter. Place the chicken atop the spinach, pour the sauce over, and serve.

flank steak with red wine sauce

6 SERVINGS

What makes this red wine sauce different is the addition of tomato paste. It gives the sauce a heartiness and depth that works perfectly with the juicy steak. Flank steak is a lean steak that should be served medium-rare; be sure to slice it rather thinly and on a sharp angle for the most tender bites.

6 TABLESPOONS (¾ STICK) COLD UNSALTED BUTTER

1 ONION, THINLY SLICED

1 TABLESPOON MINCED GARLIC

1 TEASPOON DRIED OREGANO

¼ CUP TOMATO PASTE

2½ CUPS DRY RED WINE

SALT AND FRESHLY GROUND BLACK PEPPER

2 TABLESPOONS OLIVE OIL

1 (2-POUND) FLANK STEAK OR TRI-TIP STEAKS

Melt 2 tablespoons of the butter in a large, heavy saucepan over medium-high heat. Add the onion and sauté until tender, about 5 minutes. Add the garlic and oregano and sauté until fragrant, about 30 seconds. Stir in the tomato paste and cook for 2 minutes, stirring constantly. Whisk in the wine. Simmer, stirring occasionally, until the sauce reduces by half, about 10 minutes. Remove the skillet from the heat. Whisk in the remaining 4 tablespoons of butter. Strain the sauce into a small bowl, pressing on the solids to extract as much liquid as possible. Discard the solids in the strainer. Season the sauce to taste with salt and pepper. Keep the sauce warm.

Meanwhile, heat the oil in a large, heavy skillet over medium-high heat. Sprinkle the steak generously with salt and pepper. Cook the steak to desired doneness, about 8 minutes per side for medium-rare (the steak will shrink as it cooks). Remove the skillet from the heat and let the steak rest in the skillet for 10 minutes.

Transfer the steak to a cutting board and slice it thinly across the grain. Divide the steak slices among 6 plates, drizzle the sauce over the steak, and serve.

filet mignon with balsamic syrup

Balsamic vinegar isn't just for salad dressings. Here, I reduce it to a thick and syrupy consistency to create a velvety sauce, in just minutes, that is perfect for this special cut of meat. It's luxurious without the fuss. Inexpensive vinegar works perfectly in this recipe; save the good, aged stuff for another use.

- 1½ **CUPS BALSAMIC VINEGAR**
- 3 **TABLESPOONS SUGAR**
- 2 **TABLESPOONS UNSALTED BUTTER**
- 6 **(5- TO 6-OUNCE) FILET MIGNONS (EACH ABOUT 1 INCH THICK)**
- **SALT AND FRESHLY GROUND BLACK PEPPER**
- 2 **OUNCES SOFT FRESH GOAT CHEESE**

Boil the balsamic vinegar and sugar in a small, heavy saucepan over medium-high heat until reduced to ⅓ cup, stirring occasionally, about 18 minutes.

Meanwhile, preheat the broiler. Melt the butter in a large, heavy skillet over medium-high heat. Sprinkle the steaks with salt and pepper. Cook the steaks to desired doneness, about 3 minutes per side for medium-rare. Transfer the steaks to a baking sheet. Crumble the cheese over the steaks and broil just until the cheese melts, about 1 minute. Sprinkle with pepper.

Transfer the steaks to plates. Drizzle the balsamic sauce around the steaks and serve.

rack of lamb with mint-basil pesto

6 SERVINGS

Many people consider rack of lamb a special-occasion dish: its luxurious flavor and texture and the price tag certainly warrant that. But I think that *any* family dinner is a special occasion.

- 1½ **CUPS LIGHTLY PACKED FRESH MINT LEAVES**
- ¾ **CUP LIGHTLY PACKED FRESH BASIL LEAVES**
- ½ **CUP TOASTED WALNUTS (SEE PAGE 221)**
- 2 **TABLESPOONS FRESHLY GRATED PARMESAN CHEESE**
- 2 **TABLESPOONS FRESH LEMON JUICE**
- 2 **GARLIC CLOVES**
- ¾ **TEASPOON SALT, PLUS MORE TO TASTE**
- ½ **TEASPOON FRESHLY GROUND BLACK PEPPER, PLUS MORE TO TASTE**
- ⅓ **CUP PLUS 2 TABLESPOONS OLIVE OIL**
- 3 **RACKS OF LAMB (1½ POUNDS EACH), TRIMMED**

In a food processor, blend the mint, basil, nuts, cheese, lemon juice, garlic, ¾ teaspoon salt, and ½ teaspoon pepper until the herbs are finely chopped. With the machine running, gradually blend in ⅓ cup of the oil until the pesto mixture is smooth and creamy.

Preheat the oven to 400°F. Sprinkle the lamb racks with salt and pepper. Heat the remaining 2 tablespoons oil in a large, heavy skillet over high heat. Place 1 lamb rack in the skillet and cook just until brown, about 3 minutes per side. Transfer the lamb rack meat side up on a large, heavy baking sheet. Repeat with the remaining 2 lamb racks. (The pesto and lamb may be prepared up to this point 1 day ahead. Cover the pesto and lamb separately and refrigerate. Allow an extra 5 to 8 minutes for the lamb to roast if it has been chilled.)

Roast the lamb until cooked to desired doneness, about 20 minutes for medium-rare. Transfer the lamb to a work surface to rest for 10 minutes. Cut into single chops; spread the pesto over 1 cut side of each. Arrange the chops, pesto side up, on plates, and serve.

Alternatively, the racks of lamb can be sliced, then broiled before serving. To broil the lamb: Use 18 to 24 meaty single lamb rib chops (about 2½ ounces each; from 3 racks of lamb). Preheat the broiler. Arrange the lamb chops in a single layer over 2 heavy baking sheets. Lightly brush the lamb chops with oil and sprinkle with salt and pepper. Watching closely, broil the lamb chops 3 inches from the heat source until cooked to desired doneness, about 3 minutes per side for medium-rare. Spread the pesto over the chops. Arrange the chops pesto side up on plates or a platter and serve.

veal scaloppine
with saffron cream sauce

Every cook should have a simple showstopper like this one in her repertoire. I know some of these ingredients are costly (especially the veal and the saffron) but the dish cooks in a flash and it delivers a tender, creamy, and mouthwatering bite. It's worth every penny!

1 **POUND VEAL SCALOPPINE (ABOUT 12 SLICES)**
   SALT AND FRESHLY GROUND BLACK PEPPER
2½ **TABLESPOONS UNSALTED BUTTER, OR MORE AS NEEDED**
3 **TABLESPOONS OLIVE OIL, OR MORE AS NEEDED**
12 **OUNCES CREMINI MUSHROOMS, TRIMMED AND SLICED**
2 **LARGE SHALLOTS, FINELY CHOPPED**
1 **CUP LOW-SODIUM BEEF BROTH**
¾ **CUP DRY WHITE WINE**
¼ **TEASPOON CRUMBLED SAFFRON THREADS**
¾ **CUP HEAVY CREAM**
½ **CUP FROZEN PEAS, THAWED**
4 **LEMON WEDGES**

Sprinkle the veal with salt and pepper. Melt ½ tablespoon of the butter with 2 teaspoons of the oil in a large, heavy frying pan over high heat. Working in 3 batches, add the veal and sauté until just cooked through and golden, about 45 seconds per side. Transfer the veal to a platter and tent with foil to keep it warm. Repeat with the remaining veal, adding more butter and oil to the pan as necessary.

Melt 1 tablespoon of the butter and 1 tablespoon of the oil in the same pan, over high heat. Add the mushrooms and shallots. Sprinkle with salt and pepper, and sauté until the mushrooms are golden brown, about 8 minutes. Add the broth, wine, and saffron, and simmer until the liquid reduces by half, about 5 minutes. Add the cream and boil until the sauce thickens slightly, stirring often, about 4 minutes. Add the peas and return the sauce to a simmer. Season the sauce to taste with salt and pepper.

Pour the sauce over the veal and serve with lemon wedges.

parmesan-crusted pork chops

This was my favorite way to eat pork chops as a kid. The Parmesan cheese crust makes them sensational! You can use boneless chops for this recipe; just reduce the cooking time by a minute or so.

2 **LARGE EGGS**

1 **CUP DRIED ITALIAN-STYLE BREAD CRUMBS**

¾ **CUP FRESHLY GRATED PARMESAN CHEESE**

4 **(½- TO ¾-INCH-THICK) CENTER-CUT PORK LOIN CHOPS (ABOUT 10 TO 12 OUNCES EACH)**

SALT AND FRESHLY GROUND BLACK PEPPER

6 **TABLESPOONS OLIVE OIL**

LEMON WEDGES

In a pie plate, whisk the eggs to blend. Place the bread crumbs in another pie plate. Place the cheese in a third pie plate. Sprinkle the pork chops generously with salt and pepper. Coat the chops completely with the cheese, patting to adhere. Dip the chops into the eggs, then coat completely with the bread crumbs, patting to adhere.

Heat 3 tablespoons of oil in each of 2 large, heavy skillets over medium heat. Add 2 pork chops to each skillet and cook until golden brown and just cooked through, about 5 minutes per side. Transfer the chops to plates and serve with lemon wedges.

pork chops alla pizzaiola

Pizzaiola simply refers to the sauce used on a pizza. You can use this sauce with just about anything, including chicken, beef, fish, and pasta. But this is my favorite way to use it. It's a great weeknight dinner dish and kids really seem to like it a lot.

3   TABLESPOONS EXTRA-VIRGIN OLIVE OIL

4   INCH-THICK BONE-IN CENTER-CUT PORK LOIN CHOPS (ABOUT 12 OUNCES EACH)
    SALT AND FRESHLY GROUND BLACK PEPPER

1   LARGE ONION, THINLY SLICED

1   28-OUNCE CAN DICED TOMATOES IN JUICE

2   TEASPOONS HERBES DE PROVENCE

½   TEASPOON CRUSHED DRIED RED PEPPER FLAKES, OR MORE TO TASTE

2   TABLESPOONS CHOPPED FRESH FLAT-LEAF PARSLEY

Heat 2 tablespoons of the oil in a heavy large skillet over medium heat. Sprinkle the pork chops with salt and pepper. Add 2 pork chops to the skillet and cook until they are browned and an instant read meat thermometer inserted horizontally into the chop registers 160°F, 4 to 5 minutes per side. Transfer the pork chops to a plate and tent with foil to keep them warm. Repeat with the remaining 2 pork chops, adding more oil to the pan as needed.

Add the onions to the same skillet and sauté over medium heat until crisp-tender, about 5 minutes. Add the tomatoes with their juices, herbes de Provence, and ½ teaspoon of red pepper flakes. Cover and simmer until the flavors blend and the juices thicken slightly, stirring occasionally, about 18 minutes. Season the sauce to taste with salt and more red pepper flakes if you like it spicier. Return the pork chops and any accumulated juices from the plate to the skillet and turn the pork chops to coat with the sauce. Heat until warmed through, a minute or so; do not overcook the chops.

Place 1 pork chop on each plate. Spoon the sauce over the pork chops. Sprinkle with the parsley and serve.

lasagna rolls

Here's a fun new take on lasagna that looks a little more special and serves up a little neater than your everyday version. Prosciutto and spinach make the filling much more savory and delicious than most garden-variety lasagnas. Be sure to squeeze the spinach totally dry in order to avoid a watery dish.

sauce

2   TABLESPOONS UNSALTED BUTTER

4   TEASPOONS ALL-PURPOSE FLOUR

1¼ CUPS WHOLE MILK

¼   TEASPOON SALT

⅛   TEASPOON FRESHLY GROUND BLACK PEPPER

    PINCH OF GROUND NUTMEG

lasagna

1   (15-OUNCE) CONTAINER WHOLE-MILK RICOTTA CHEESE

1   (10-OUNCE) BOX FROZEN CHOPPED SPINACH, THAWED
    AND SQUEEZED DRY

1   CUP PLUS 2 TABLESPOONS FRESHLY GRATED PARMESAN CHEESE

3   OUNCES THINLY SLICED PROSCIUTTO, CHOPPED

1   LARGE EGG, LIGHTLY BEATEN

¾   TEASPOON SALT, PLUS MORE FOR PASTA

½   TEASPOON FRESHLY GROUND BLACK PEPPER

12 DRIED LASAGNA NOODLES

    BUTTER, FOR BAKING DISH

2   CUPS QUICK MARINARA SAUCE (PAGE 144)

1   CUP SHREDDED MOZZARELLA CHEESE (ABOUT 4 OUNCES)

to make the sauce

Melt the butter in a medium, heavy saucepan over medium-low heat. Add the flour and cook for 3 minutes, whisking continuously. Whisk in the milk. Increase the heat to medium-high. Whisk the sauce until it comes to a simmer and is thick and smooth, about 3 minutes. Whisk the salt, pepper, and nutmeg into the cream sauce.

(recipe continues)

to make the lasagna

In a medium bowl, stir together the ricotta, spinach, 1 cup of the Parmesan cheese, prosciutto, egg, the ¾ teaspoon of salt, and the pepper until blended.

Bring a very large pot of salted water to a boil over high heat. Add the lasagna noodles and cook until just tender but still firm to the bite, stirring frequently to prevent the noodles from sticking together. Drain. Arrange the noodles in a single layer on a baking sheet to prevent them from sticking.

Preheat the oven to 450°F. Butter a 13 × 9 × 2-inch glass baking dish. Spread the cream sauce over the bottom of the prepared dish.

Lay out 4 lasagna noodles on a work surface, then spread about 3 tablespoons of the ricotta mixture evenly over each noodle. Roll the noodles up and arrange the rolls, seam sides down and not touching one another, atop the cream sauce. Repeat with the remaining noodles and ricotta mixture. Spoon 1 cup of the marinara sauce over the lasagna rolls, then sprinkle with the mozzarella and remaining 2 tablespoons of Parmesan cheese. Cover the dish tightly with foil. Bake until the rolls are heated through and the sauce bubbles, about 20 minutes. Uncover and bake until the cheese on top is golden, about 15 minutes longer. Let stand for 10 minutes.

Meanwhile, heat the remaining marinara sauce in a small, heavy saucepan over medium heat until hot. Transfer the sauce to a sauceboat and serve alongside.

stuffed zucchini and red bell peppers

This festive, beautiful dish makes for an unusual entrée or even a substantial side with a simple baked pasta. Feel free to substitute ground beef for the turkey, or omit the meats entirely for a vegetarian version.

OLIVE OIL, FOR BAKING DISH

1 SMALL ONION, GRATED

¼ CUP CHOPPED FRESH FLAT-LEAF PARSLEY

1 LARGE EGG

3 TABLESPOONS KETCHUP

3 GARLIC CLOVES, MINCED

1 TEASPOON SALT

¼ TEASPOON FRESHLY GROUND BLACK PEPPER

⅓ CUP GRATED PECORINO ROMANO CHEESE

¼ CUP PLAIN DRIED BREAD CRUMBS

1 POUND GROUND TURKEY

2 ZUCCHINI, HALVED LENGTHWISE

1 SHORT ORANGE BELL PEPPER, HALVED CROSSWISE AND SEEDED

1 SHORT RED BELL PEPPER, HALVED CROSSWISE AND SEEDED

1 SHORT YELLOW BELL PEPPER, HALVED CROSSWISE AND SEEDED

1½ CUPS QUICK MARINARA SAUCE (PAGE 144)

Preheat the oven to 400°F. Lightly oil a 13 × 9 × 2-inch baking dish.

In a large bowl, whisk the onion, parsley, egg, ketchup, garlic, salt, and pepper to blend. Stir in the cheese and bread crumbs, then, using your hands, mix in the turkey. Cover the turkey mixture and refrigerate.

Using a melon baller or spoon, carefully scrape out the seeds and inner flesh from the zucchini, leaving ⅛-inch-thick shells. Be careful not to pierce the skin. Fill the zucchini and pepper halves with the turkey mixture, dividing equally and mounding slightly. Arrange the stuffed vegetables in the prepared baking dish. Spoon the marinara sauce over the stuffed vegetables.

Bake uncovered until the vegetables are tender and beginning to brown and a thermometer inserted into the filling registers 165°F, about 45 minutes. Transfer the stuffed vegetables to a platter and serve.

the italian
GRILL

Americans certainly love their grills, but grilling
isn't an exclusively American pastime. It's also an Italian mainstay, especially in the South. Summertime in Sicily means fresh-caught fish on the grill, with just a hint of seasoning. Grilling imparts a remarkable and unique flavor that works wonders on a surprising variety of dishes. Meats are naturals for the grill, and I don't just mean hamburgers: try my grilled lamb with salsa verde for a whole new spin on barbecuing. Some unexpected ingredients also come alive with a grill's smoky flavor, like lettuce and even fruit. Grilling is always a crowd-pleaser, and even if you don't have a yard, grill pans make a fine substitute, any time of the year.

PANE ALLA GRILLIA

GRILLED PORTOBELLO MUSHROOMS WITH TOMATOES
AND FRESH MOZZARELLA

GRILLED LETTUCES

GRILLED ARTICHOKES WITH PARSLEY AND GARLIC

GRILLED STEAK SANDWICHES

GRILLED CHICKEN WITH GREMOLATA

GRILLED CHICKEN WITH BASIL DRESSING

GRILLED LAMB WITH SALSA VERDE

GRILLED TUNA BURGERS WITH TAPENADE

SWORDFISH SPIEDINI

GRILLED TUNA STEAKS WITH ROASTED CIPOLLINI ONIONS

GRILLED SUMMER FRUIT

ITALIAN S'MORES

CHARCOAL GRILLING

Here are my pointers for successful grilling:

Place a handful of newspaper in a charcoal chimney and top with about twenty-five pieces of natural lump oakwood charcoal. Stand the charcoal chimney on a nonflammable surface. Light the paper through the hole near the bottom of the chimney and let the charcoal burn until the ash is gray, about 30 minutes.

Open the vents on the bottom of the barbecue and on the lid, and remove the top grill rack. Carefully shake the hot charcoal over the bottom of the grill. Return the rack and the lid to the barbecue. Allow the charcoal fire to heat the grill rack so that it is very hot before placing food on it.

To check the heat of the charcoal fire, hold your hand 5 inches above the grill rack. It is a high heat if you can hold your hand above the rack for just 1 or 2 seconds, a medium-high heat if you can hold your hand above the rack for 3 or 4 seconds, and a medium-low heat if you can hold your hand above the rack for 5 or 6 seconds.

pane alla grillia

{GRILLED BREAD}

6 SERVINGS

This is perfect for dipping in soups and stews, as a side, or just as a great way to use up day-old bread, which is exactly how this recipe was born.

- 6 (½- TO ¾-INCH-THICK) SLICES CIABATTA
  OR OTHER COUNTRY-STYLE WHITE BREAD
- 1½ TABLESPOONS OLIVE OIL
- 2 LARGE GARLIC CLOVES
- 1 TOMATO, HALVED CROSSWISE
  SALT AND FRESHLY GROUND BLACK PEPPER

Prepare a charcoal or gas grill for medium-high heat or preheat a ridged grill pan over medium-high heat. Brush both cut sides of the ciabatta slices with the oil. Grill the ciabatta slices until they are golden and crisp, about 2 minutes per side. Rub the toasted surfaces of the bread with the garlic cloves, then rub with the cut side of the tomatoes. Sprinkle with salt and pepper, and serve warm.

grilled portobello mushrooms with tomatoes and fresh mozzarella

4 SERVINGS

It's easy enough to grill the steaklike portobellos, and the elegant presentation turns the incredibly simple prep work into a snazzy first course or side dish. I like to serve this when I have a vegetarian guest at my barbecue, because the meaty mushrooms are substantial enough to satisfy those who are passing on the burgers.

4   LARGE PORTOBELLO MUSHROOMS
     (ABOUT 5 INCHES IN DIAMETER), STEMMED

3   TABLESPOONS OLIVE OIL

    SALT AND FRESHLY GROUND BLACK PEPPER

3   TABLESPOONS EXTRA-VIRGIN OLIVE OIL

½   TEASPOON MINCED GARLIC

2   RIPE TOMATOES, CUT INTO ½-INCH PIECES

8   OUNCES FRESH WATER-PACKED MOZZARELLA,
    DRAINED AND CUT INTO ½-INCH CUBES

¼   CUP CHOPPED FRESH BASIL

Prepare a charcoal or gas grill for medium-high heat or preheat a ridged grill pan over medium-high heat. Brush the mushrooms on both sides with the olive oil and sprinkle with salt and pepper. Grill until the mushrooms are heated through and tender, about 5 minutes per side.

Meanwhile, in a medium bowl, whisk the extra-virgin olive oil and garlic to blend. Add the tomatoes, cheese, and basil, and toss to coat. Season the tomato salad to taste with salt and pepper.

Place 1 hot grilled mushroom gill side up on each of 4 plates. Sprinkle with more salt and pepper. Spoon the tomato salad atop the mushrooms and serve.

"Some unexpected ingredients come alive with a grill."

grilled lettuces

6 SERVINGS

Surprisingly, lettuce is fabulous grilled! If you're bored of the same old salads, try this one; it's really special and different.

- 3 TABLESPOONS OLIVE OIL
- 3 HEADS OF BELGIAN ENDIVE, HALVED LENGTHWISE
- 1 LARGE HEAD OF RADICCHIO, CUT INTO 6 WEDGES
- 1 HEAD OF ROMAINE LETTUCE, QUARTERED
- SALT AND FRESHLY GROUND BLACK PEPPER
- 2 TABLESPOONS BALSAMIC VINEGAR

Prepare a charcoal or gas grill for medium-high heat or preheat a ridged grill pan over medium-high heat. Brush 1 tablespoon of the oil over the endive, radicchio, and romaine, then sprinkle with salt and pepper. Grill the lettuces, turning occasionally, until they are crisp-tender and browned in spots, about 6 minutes. Coarsely chop the lettuces, then toss them in a large bowl with the vinegar and remaining 2 tablespoons of oil. Season the salad to taste with more salt and pepper. Serve warm.

grilled artichokes with parsley and garlic

6 TO 8 SERVINGS

I know that many people are intimidated by artichokes, but honestly, preparing them sounds more complicated than it is. There are a couple of tricks to keep in mind, though: use a sharp knife to cut through the tough stem and leaves, and use plenty of lemon juice to keep the cut surfaces from getting oxidized and turning dark. I promise, the time you spend prepping the 'chokes will be worth it.

2   LEMONS, HALVED

6   LARGE ARTICHOKES

⅓   CUP FRESH LEMON JUICE

3   TABLESPOONS CHOPPED FRESH FLAT-LEAF PARSLEY

1   TEASPOON MINCED GARLIC

1   TEASPOON SALT

½   TEASPOON FRESHLY GROUND BLACK PEPPER

½   CUP EXTRA-VIRGIN OLIVE OIL

Squeeze the juice from the halved lemons into a large bowl of cold water. Trim the stem of 1 artichoke to about 1 inch long. Bend back and snap off the outer dark green leaves until the pale greenish-yellow inner leaves are visible. Cut off the top inch of the artichoke to remove any dark green tops and sharp points from the remaining leaves. Using a vegetable peeler, peel the tough, dark green areas from the stem and base of the artichoke. Quarter the artichoke lengthwise. Using a small sharp knife, cut out the choke and remove any purple prickly-tipped leaves from the center of each artichoke wedge. Drop the trimmed wedges into the lemon water. Trim the remaining artichokes in the same fashion.

Bring a large pot of salted water to a boil. Drain the artichokes, add to the boiling water, and boil until crisp-tender, about 12 minutes. Drain. Transfer the artichokes to a rack and cool. (The artichokes can be prepared up to this point 1 day in advance. Cover and refrigerate them until you are ready to grill.)

Prepare a charcoal or gas grill for medium-high heat or preheat a ridged grill pan over medium-high heat. Whisk the ⅓ cup of lemon juice, parsley, garlic, salt, and pepper in a bowl. Gradually whisk in the oil. Brush the artichokes with some of the dressing. Grill the artichokes until tender and lightly charred in spots, turning occasionally, about 10 minutes. Transfer the grilled artichokes to a platter and drizzle with the remaining dressing. Serve warm or at room temperature.

grilled steak sandwiches

These are perfect for a casual Sunday barbecue. All the ingredients can be prepped ahead and a little bit of meat goes a long way.

¼	CUP BALSAMIC VINEGAR
¼	CUP SOY SAUCE
¼	CUP WORCESTERSHIRE SAUCE
1	TABLESPOON YELLOW MUSTARD SEEDS, CRACKED
2	(12- TO 14-OUNCE) RIB-EYE STEAKS
4	OUNCES GORGONZOLA CHEESE, CRUMBLED
½	CUP SOUR CREAM
	SALT AND FRESHLY GROUND BLACK PEPPER
1	BAGUETTE (ABOUT 2 FEET LONG), SPLIT LENGTHWISE
2	CUPS LIGHTLY PACKED ARUGULA

In a large resealable plastic bag, combine the vinegar, soy sauce, Worcestershire sauce, and mustard seeds. Add the steaks and seal the bag. Refrigerate for at least 30 minutes and up to 2 hours, turning the steaks occasionally.

Prepare a charcoal or gas grill for medium-high heat or preheat a ridged grill pan over medium-high heat. Drain the marinade from the steaks. Grill the steaks to desired doneness, about 6 minutes per side for medium-rare. Let the steaks rest for 10 minutes, then cut them crosswise into thin slices.

Meanwhile, stir the cheese and sour cream in a small bowl to form a thick spread. Season the cheese mixture to taste with salt and pepper. Remove some of the bread from the center of the baguette halves. Spread the cheese mixture over the baguette halves. Arrange the arugula and even amounts of the warm steak slices on the bottom piece of bread. Sprinkle the steak slices with salt and pepper. Cover with the baguette top. Cut the sandwich crosswise into 6 equal pieces and serve.

grilled chicken with gremolata

4 SERVINGS

Gremolata, or *gremolada,* is spelled differently depending on the region of Italy. It's a paste made of chopped fresh herbs, garlic, and citrus zest that can be sprinkled or smeared on just about any finished dish. It's the traditional accompaniment to osso buco but it brings a bright, fresh flavor to meat, poultry, or fish. I love it on grilled chicken!

¼ CUP FINELY CHOPPED FRESH FLAT-LEAF PARSLEY

2 TABLESPOONS EXTRA-VIRGIN OLIVE OIL

1½ TABLESPOONS LEMON ZEST

1 TEASPOON FINELY CHOPPED FRESH OREGANO

1 TEASPOON FINELY CHOPPED GARLIC

1 TEASPOON OLIVE OIL

4 (6-OUNCE) BONELESS CHICKEN BREAST HALVES WITH SKIN

SALT AND FRESHLY GROUND BLACK PEPPER

In a small bowl, combine the parsley, extra-virgin olive oil, lemon zest, oregano, and garlic. Set the gremolata aside.

Prepare a charcoal or gas grill for medium-high heat or preheat a ridged grill pan over medium-high heat. Rub the olive oil over both sides of the chicken. Sprinkle the chicken with salt and pepper. Grill until just cooked through, about 5 minutes per side. Transfer the chicken to a platter. Immediately spoon the gremolata over the chicken, and serve.

grilled chicken with basil dressing

Grilled chicken cutlets are easy and beautiful, but they do have a tendency to dry out, so marinating them will help keep them moist, tender, and flavorful on the grill. The basil dressing gives them added freshness and lightens them up!

- ⅔ **CUP EXTRA-VIRGIN OLIVE OIL**
- 3 **TABLESPOONS PLUS ¼ CUP FRESH LEMON JUICE (FROM ABOUT 4 LEMONS)**
- 1½ **TEASPOONS FENNEL SEEDS, COARSELY CRUSHED**
- 1½ **TEASPOONS SALT, PLUS MORE TO TASTE**
- 1 **TEASPOON FRESHLY GROUND BLACK PEPPER, PLUS MORE TO TASTE**
- 6 **BONELESS, SKINLESS CHICKEN BREAST HALVES**
- 1 **CUP LIGHTLY PACKED FRESH BASIL LEAVES**
- 1 **LARGE GARLIC CLOVE**
- 1 **TEASPOON GRATED LEMON ZEST**

In a resealable plastic bag, combine ⅓ cup of the oil, 3 tablespoons of the lemon juice, the fennel seeds, ¾ teaspoon of the salt, and ½ teaspoon of the pepper. Add the chicken and seal the bag. Massage the marinade into the chicken. Refrigerate for at least 30 minutes and up to 24 hours, turning the chicken occasionally.

Meanwhile, in a blender, blend the basil, garlic, lemon zest, remaining ¼ cup lemon juice, ¾ teaspoon salt, and ½ teaspoon pepper until smooth. Gradually blend in the remaining ⅓ cup oil. Season the basil sauce to taste with more salt and pepper, if desired.

Prepare a charcoal or gas grill for medium-high heat or preheat a ridged grill pan over medium-high heat. Grill the chicken until just cooked through, about 5 minutes per side. Transfer the chicken to a platter. Drizzle with the basil sauce and serve.

grilled lamb with salsa verde

I love grilled lamb with mint. Smoky, charry grilled lamb with fresh mint is a springtime treat.

1 CUP OLIVE OIL, PREFERABLY EXTRA-VIRGIN

½ CUP FRESH LEMON JUICE (FROM ABOUT 4 LEMONS)

½ CUP CHOPPED FRESH FLAT-LEAF PARSLEY

⅓ CUP CHOPPED SCALLIONS

¼ CUP CHOPPED FRESH MINT

¼ CUP SALTED CAPERS, SOAKED FOR 30 MINUTES, DRAINED AND COARSELY CHOPPED

2 TEASPOONS GRATED LEMON ZEST

½ TEASPOON CRUSHED DRIED RED PEPPER FLAKES

3½ TEASPOONS COARSE SALT

1½ TEASPOONS FRESHLY GROUND BLACK PEPPER

1 (4 ½- TO 5-POUND) BONED AND BUTTERFLIED LEG OF LAMB

1 TABLESPOON MINCED GARLIC

NONSTICK COOKING SPRAY

In a large bowl, stir the oil, lemon juice, parsley, scallions, mint, capers, lemon zest, and red pepper flakes to blend. Whisk in 1½ teaspoons of the salt and ½ teaspoon of the black pepper. Set the salsa verde aside.

Place the lamb in a 15 × 10 × 2-inch glass baking dish. Rub the remaining 2 teaspoons of salt, 1 teaspoon of black pepper, and the garlic all over the lamb. Pour ½ cup of salsa verde over the lamb, turning to coat it evenly. (At this point you may cover the dish and remaining salsa verde separately with plastic wrap and refrigerate up to 1 day.)

Spray a grill rack with nonstick spray and prepare a charcoal or gas grill for medium-high heat, or preheat a large rectangular ridged grill pan over medium-high heat. Grill the lamb, turning occasionally, until a meat thermometer inserted into the thicker parts registers 130°F for medium-rare, about 40 minutes. Transfer the lamb to a work surface and let it rest for 15 minutes.

Cut the lamb across the grain into thin slices. Arrange the lamb slices on a platter and drizzle with some of the reserved salsa verde. Serve the remaining salsa verde alongside.

grilled tuna burgers with tapenade

This is the perfect alternative to beef burgers. You could substitute salmon for the tuna if it's easier to come by. This tastes great at room temperature, so pack it along on picnics.

⅓ **CUP PITTED GREEN OLIVES**

¼ **CUP PITTED KALAMATA OLIVES**

1 **TABLESPOON DRAINED CAPERS**

1 **TABLESPOON PLUS 2 TEASPOONS EXTRA-VIRGIN OLIVE OIL**

1 **TABLESPOON FRESH LEMON JUICE**

1 **TABLESPOON CHOPPED FRESH FLAT-LEAF PARSLEY**

1 **TEASPOON LEMON ZEST**

1 **ANCHOVY, MINCED**

FRESHLY GROUND BLACK PEPPER

⅓ **CUP MAYONNAISE**

2 **TABLESPOONS DIJON MUSTARD**

1 **(12- TO 14-OUNCE) TUNA STEAK**

SALT

1 **BAGUETTE (ABOUT 2 FEET LONG), HALVED HORIZONTALLY AND QUARTERED INTO 6-INCH-LONG SEGMENTS**

4 **ROMAINE LETTUCE LEAVES**

4 **THIN SLICES OF RED ONION**

½ **CUP PURCHASED ROASTED RED PEPPERS, DRAINED**

In a food processor, combine the green and kalamata olives, capers, 1 tablespoon of the oil, the lemon juice, parsley, lemon zest, and anchovy. Pulse just until the olives are finely chopped. Season the tapenade with pepper.

Stir the mayonnaise and mustard in a small bowl to blend. (The tapenade and mustard-mayonnaise mixture can be prepared 1 day ahead. Cover separately and refrigerate. Bring the tapenade to room temperature before using.)

Prepare a charcoal or gas grill for medium-high heat or preheat a ridged grill pan over medium-high heat. Lightly brush the tuna with the remaining 2 teaspoons of oil. Sprinkle with salt and pepper. Grill the tuna until golden on the outside and just opaque in the center, about 2 minutes per side. Remove some of the bread from the center of each baguette piece. Grill the baguette pieces, cut side down, until lightly toasted, about 2 minutes.

Spread the mayonnaise mixture over the bottom and top halves of the baguette pieces. Arrange a layer of lettuce and red onion on the bottom halves. Cut the tuna steaks into ½-inch-thick slices. Arrange the tuna slices over the onion. Spoon the tapenade over the tuna. Top with the red peppers then the baguette tops, and serve.

swordfish spiedini

Spiedini is the Italian word for "kebabs." When I went sailing around the Sicilian islands a number of years ago, we ate a lot of swordfish because the sea there is filled with them. The combination of fish and pancetta was one of my favorites, not only because I love the meaty flavor with the lightness of the fish but because it is a beautiful presentation that makes a little bit of fish go a long way. If you don't have swordfish, halibut is a good substitute, and bacon can stand in for the pancetta.

- 2 TABLESPOONS OLIVE OIL
- 1 TO 2 TEASPOONS HERBES DE PROVENCE
- ½ TEASPOON SALT
- ½ TEASPOON FRESHLY GROUND BLACK PEPPER
- 1½ POUNDS SWORDFISH STEAK, TRIMMED AND CUT INTO 1-INCH PIECES
- 6 THIN SLICES PANCETTA OR BACON
- 6 METAL OR WOODEN SKEWERS SOAKED IN WATER 30 MINUTES

Prepare a charcoal or gas grill for medium-high heat or preheat a ridged grill pan over medium-high heat. In a large bowl, whisk the oil, herbes de Provence, salt, and pepper to blend. Add the swordfish cubes and toss to coat. Thread the swordfish cubes alternately with 1 slice of pancetta onto each of the skewers, wrapping the pancetta around the fish cubes as you go.

Grill the skewers until the swordfish is just opaque in the center and the pancetta is crisp, about 8 minutes, turning and brushing often with the remaining marinade.

grilled tuna steaks with roasted cipollini onions

Tuna is a hearty fish and my favorite way to cook it is on the grill; it doesn't fall apart and I love the smoky flavors. Cipollini onions are sweeter and more tender than regular onions, and roasted in the oven they're even sweeter. The sweet-tart flavor is a nice counterpoint to the slightly bland fish.

If you can't find cipollini onions, try pearl onions. They cook in about half the time but the flavor is not as sophisticated.

2 **POUNDS CIPOLLINI ONIONS**

⅔ **CUP BALSAMIC VINEGAR**

1 **TABLESPOON PLUS ⅓ CUP EXTRA-VIRGIN OLIVE OIL**

1 **TEASPOON SALT**

½ **TEASPOON FRESHLY GROUND BLACK PEPPER**

3 **TABLESPOONS FRESH LEMON JUICE**

2 **TEASPOONS CHOPPED FRESH THYME**

6 **(6-OUNCE) TUNA STEAKS (1 INCH THICK)**

Bring a large pot of water to a boil. Add the onions and cook for 2 minutes. Drain and cool. Peel the onions and cut off the root ends.

Preheat the oven to 450°F. Toss the onions, vinegar, 1 tablespoon of the oil, ½ teaspoon of the salt, and ¼ teaspoon of the pepper in a 13 × 9 × 2-inch baking dish. Roast in the oven, stirring occasionally, until the onions are tender and golden, about 1 hour.

Meanwhile, whisk the remaining ⅓ cup of oil, the lemon juice, thyme, and remaining ½ teaspoon of salt and ¼ teaspoon of pepper in another 13 × 9 × 2-inch baking dish. Place the tuna steaks in the marinade and turn to coat. Let stand for 5 minutes on each side.

Oil a grill rack and prepare a charcoal or gas grill for medium-high heat, or preheat a ridged grill pan over medium-high heat. Grill the steaks to desired doneness, about 3 minutes per side for medium. Cut the steaks in half and transfer to a platter. Spoon the onion mixture around the tuna steaks and serve.

grilled summer fruit

6 SERVINGS

Grilling fruit is a wonderful way to enhance its sweet flavor. The heat from the grill brings out the natural sugars in the fruit to create a sugary crust. The type of fruit you use is up to you (figs are also great cooked this way), but these are some of the ones I like most. The alternating colors make the skewers especially pretty.

NONSTICK COOKING SPRAY

3 FIRM BUT RIPE NECTARINES, HALVED AND PITTED

3 FIRM BUT RIPE PLUMS, HALVED AND PITTED

3 FIRM BUT RIPE APRICOTS, HALVED AND PITTED

6 METAL OR WOODEN SKEWERS SOAKED IN WATER 30 MINUTES

3 TABLESPOONS SUGAR

VANILLA ICE CREAM (OPTIONAL)

Spray a grill rack with nonstick spray and prepare a charcoal or gas grill for medium-high heat, or preheat a ridged grill pan over medium-high heat. Thread 1 piece of each fruit on each of 6 skewers so that the cut sides line up and lie flat. Sprinkle the sugar over the cut sides of the fruit. Let them stand until the sugar dissolves, about 10 minutes.

Place the fruit skewers on the grill cut side down. Grill the fruit until it is heated through and caramelized, about 5 minutes. Place 1 fruit skewer on each plate and serve with a scoop of ice cream, if you like.

italian s'mores

MAKES 12

Everyone grew up on this traditional campfire favorite—graham crackers, toasted marsh-mallows, and melted chocolate. As kids we didn't have graham crackers in our pantry; we did have lots of bread, though, so I improvised this Italianized version of an American dessert classic.

- 2 **TABLESPOONS SUGAR**
- 12 **(½-INCH-THICK) BAGUETTE SLICES, CUT ON THE DIAGONAL**
- 3 **TABLESPOONS UNSALTED BUTTER, MELTED**
- 2 **(3-OUNCE) BARS GIANDUJA CHOCOLATE OR SEMISWEET CHOCOLATE WITH HAZELNUTS, BROKEN INTO SQUARES**
- 24 **LARGE MARSHMALLOWS**
- 6 **METAL OR WOODEN SKEWERS SOAKED IN WATER 30 MINUTES**

Remove the grill rack from a charcoal or gas grill and preheat the grill for medium-high heat. Preheat the oven to 350°F. Line a large baking sheet with parchment paper or foil. Place the sugar on a small plate. Arrange the bread slices on the baking sheet. Generously brush the butter over the bread slices. Dip the bread slices, butter side down, into the sugar. Return the bread slices, sugar side up, to the baking sheet. Bake until the crostini are crisp and golden, about 15 minutes. Immediately arrange the chocolate pieces in a single layer atop the crostini.

Meanwhile, thread 2 marshmallows onto each of the skewers. Roast the marshmallows directly over the grill flames or stovetop flames until toasted to desired doneness. Push 2 roasted marshmallows onto the chocolate on each crostini and serve. Repeat to make 12 s'mores total.

alternative: Chocolate-hazelnut spread (such as Nutella) may be used in place of the choco-late bars. Omit coating the bread slices with sugar before baking them, and spread about 2 teaspoons of the chocolate-hazelnut spread over each crostini before topping it with the roasted marshmallows.

family-style
PASTA

For a casual get-together, Italians know that
there's nothing more satisfying—or economical—to set on the table than a big bowl piled high with pasta. Everyone can serve themselves as much as they want, and it can be either a side dish or a main course. There are so many different kinds of pasta to experiment with; if you haven't ventured much beyond spaghetti and linguine, you've missed out. The recipes that follow will help you break out of your pasta rut with new shapes and new flavors (I especially love whole wheat pastas these days). People often tell me they avoid making pasta because it always ends up sticky or gummy, but I tell them to remember one secret: make sure the pot is big enough for the pasta to "swim" in the water. That way, your pasta will be perfect every time.

LITTLE THIMBLES SCIUE' SCIUE'

LINGUINE WITH CHICKEN RAGÙ

FRESH FETTUCCINE WITH ROASTED CHICKEN
AND BROCCOLI RABE

PENNE WITH SPINACH SAUCE

CHICKEN CARBONARA

POLPETTE AND SPAGHETTI

RIGATONI WITH STEAK

FUSILLI WITH SHRIMP AND ARUGULA

QUICK MARINARA SAUCE

RAVIOLI WITH CREAMY TOMATO SAUCE

PENNE WITH SAUSAGE, ARTICHOKES,
AND SUN-DRIED TOMATOES

WHOLE WHEAT SPAGHETTI WITH SWISS CHARD
AND PECORINO CHEESE

FARFALLE WITH ASPARAGUS AND MUSHROOMS

RED WINE RISOTTO WITH PEAS

DIRTY RISOTTO

"Vine-ripened tomatoes make the freshest sauces."

little thimbles sciue' sciue'

8 (½-CUP) SERVINGS

This dish was one I had often when growing up. *Sciue' sciue'* means "improvisation," so basically you put whatever you want in the pasta and make your own *sciue' scuie'.* This was and is a staple recipe of my grandfather, who was born in Naples, where they grow abundant quantities of tomatoes. His was a pasta-making family and these ingredients were always leftovers; they became our *sciue' sciue'.*

> SALT
>
> 1½ CUPS (ABOUT 6 OUNCES) DITALINI (THIMBLE-SHAPED PASTA) OR OTHER SMALL TUBE-SHAPED PASTA, SUCH AS ELBOW MACARONI OR *PENNETTE*
>
> 2 TABLESPOONS OLIVE OIL
>
> 3 GARLIC CLOVES, MINCED
>
> 5 PLUM TOMATOES (ABOUT 1 POUND), CORED AND CHOPPED
>
> 8 OUNCES FRESH MOZZARELLA CHEESE, DRAINED AND CUT INTO ½-INCH CUBES
>
> 8 LARGE FRESH BASIL LEAVES, COARSELY CHOPPED

Bring a large saucepan of salted water to a boil. Add the ditalini and cook, stirring often to prevent the pasta from sticking together, until tender but still firm to the bite, about 8 minutes. Drain.

Meanwhile, in a large, heavy skillet, heat the oil over medium heat. Add the garlic and sauté until fragrant, about 1 minute. Add the tomatoes and sauté just until heated through, about 2 minutes. Add the cooked pasta. Remove the skillet from the heat. Add the cheese and basil, and toss to coat. Season the pasta to taste with salt. Spoon the pasta into small serving bowls and serve immediately.

linguine with chicken ragù

Ragùs are classic Italian sauces that are generally made from rich, less tender cuts of meat and cooked slowly for a long time to develop the flavors and tenderize the meat. I use chicken thighs because they give that intensely rich taste without the guilt and in a fraction of the time.

2	**TABLESPOONS OLIVE OIL**
1½	**POUNDS BONELESS, SKINLESS CHICKEN THIGHS, FINELY CHOPPED**
½	**CUP FINELY CHOPPED SHALLOTS**
1	**TABLESPOON MINCED GARLIC**
2	**TEASPOONS FINELY CHOPPED FRESH ROSEMARY**
⅔	**CUP DRY WHITE WINE**
4	**CUPS QUICK MARINARA SAUCE (PAGE 144)**
	SALT
1	**POUND DRIED LINGUINE**
½	**CUP FRESHLY GRATED PARMESAN CHEESE**

Heat the oil in a large, heavy skillet over medium-high heat. Add the chopped chicken and cook until the juices evaporate and the chicken is golden, about 10 minutes. Add the shallots, garlic, and rosemary, and sauté until tender, about 2 minutes. Add the wine and stir to scrape up any brown bits on the bottom of the skillet. Add the marinara sauce. Bring to a simmer. Reduce the heat to medium-low and simmer gently until the flavors blend, about 10 minutes.

Meanwhile, bring a large pot of salted water to a boil. Add the linguine and cook, stirring often to prevent the pasta from sticking together, until tender but still firm to the bite, about 8 minutes. Drain, reserving 1 cup of cooking liquid. Add the linguine to the ragù and toss to coat, adding some reserved cooking liquid to moisten.

Transfer the pasta to a large serving bowl, sprinkle with Parmesan cheese, and serve.

fresh fettuccine with roasted chicken and broccoli rabe

4 MAIN-COURSE SERVINGS

When you're in a rush to get dinner on the table, take some shortcuts. I did, which is how this dish came to be. What did we ever do before fresh rotisserie-roasted chickens were readily available at every market? Here's a different way to use this weeknight standby, combining it with bitter broccoli rabe and fresh pasta from the dairy case, which cooks in just minutes.

SALT

1 POUND BROCCOLI RABE, TRIMMED AND STALKS CUT CROSSWISE INTO 3-INCH PIECES

1 (9-OUNCE) PACKAGE FRESH FETTUCCINE

1 (14-OUNCE) CAN REDUCED-SODIUM CHICKEN BROTH

¼ CUP FRESH LEMON JUICE (FROM ABOUT 2 LEMONS)

3 CUPS SHREDDED ROASTED CHICKEN (1 ROASTED CHICKEN WILL YIELD 3 TO 4 CUPS OF SHREDDED MEAT)

¾ CUP FRESHLY GRATED PARMESAN CHEESE

½ CUP TOASTED PINE NUTS (SEE PAGE 221)

2 TABLESPOONS CHOPPED FRESH FLAT-LEAF PARSLEY

2 TABLESPOONS OLIVE OIL

1 TABLESPOON LEMON ZEST

FRESHLY GROUND BLACK PEPPER

Bring a large pot of salted water to a boil. Add the broccoli rabe and cook until crisp-tender, 2 minutes. Using a slotted spoon, transfer the broccoli rabe to a large bowl. Add the fettuccine to the same pot of boiling water and cook, stirring to prevent the pasta from sticking together, until just tender, about 2 minutes. Drain, reserving ½ cup of the cooking liquid.

Meanwhile, in a large, heavy skillet, bring the broth and lemon juice to a boil over medium-high heat. Boil until the broth is reduced by half, about 5 minutes. Add the chicken and simmer just until heated through, about 2 minutes. Add the pasta, broccoli rabe, ½ cup of the Parmesan cheese, the pine nuts, parsley, oil, and lemon zest. Toss to coat, adding some of the reserved cooking liquid ¼ cup at a time to moisten, and season to taste with salt and pepper.

Mound the pasta into bowls, sprinkle with the remaining ¼ cup Parmesan cheese, and serve.

penne with spinach sauce

4 MAIN-COURSE SERVINGS OR 6 SIDE-DISH SERVINGS

The thing that's great about this pasta is that there's really no cooking aside from boiling the pasta; just throw all the sauce ingredients right into the food processor while the pasta cooks.

¾ TEASPOON SALT, PLUS MORE TO TASTE

1 POUND WHOLE WHEAT OR MULTIGRAIN PENNE

3 GARLIC CLOVES

2 OUNCES GOAT CHEESE

1 OUNCE REDUCED-FAT CREAM CHEESE

½ TEASPOON FRESHLY GROUND BLACK PEPPER, PLUS MORE TO TASTE

6 OUNCES BABY SPINACH LEAVES

2 TABLESPOONS FRESHLY GRATED PARMESAN CHEESE

Bring a large pot of salted water to a boil. Add the penne and cook, stirring occasionally, until it is tender but still firm to the bite, about 12 minutes. Drain, reserving 1 cup of the cooking liquid.

While the pasta cooks, mince the garlic in a food processor. Add the goat cheese, cream cheese, ¾ teaspoon of salt, ½ teaspoon of pepper, and half of the spinach leaves. Blend until the mixture is smooth and creamy. Place the remaining spinach leaves in a large bowl. Add the drained pasta, then scrape the cheese mixture over the pasta and toss to coat, adding enough reserved cooking liquid to moisten. Season the pasta to taste with salt and pepper. Sprinkle with the Parmesan cheese and serve.

chicken carbonara

The traditional carbonara is made of eggs, pancetta, Parmesan cheese, and spaghetti, but in an effort to make a more substantial meal, I threw in some leftover chicken, walnuts, and lemon zest, and it became a hit. And sometimes that's just how it works.

- 2 **TEASPOONS OLIVE OIL**
- 4 **OUNCES THINLY SLICED PANCETTA OR BACON, CHOPPED**
- 2½ **CUPS WHIPPING CREAM**
- 1 **CUP FRESHLY GRATED PARMESAN CHEESE**
- 8 **LARGE EGG YOLKS**
- ¼ **CUP CHOPPED FRESH BASIL**
- ¼ **CUP CHOPPED FRESH FLAT-LEAF PARSLEY**
- 2 **TEASPOONS MINCED GARLIC**
- 4 **CUPS COARSELY SHREDDED CHICKEN (FROM 1 ROASTED CHICKEN)**
  SALT
- 1 **POUND SPAGHETTI**
  FRESHLY GROUND BLACK PEPPER
- ½ **CUP TOASTED WALNUTS, CHOPPED (SEE PAGE 221)**
- 1 **TABLESPOON FINELY GRATED LEMON ZEST**

Heat the oil in a large, heavy frying pan over medium heat. Add the pancetta and sauté until it is brown and crisp, about 8 minutes. Cool until lukewarm. Whisk in the cream, cheese, yolks, basil, parsley, and garlic. Stir in the chicken.

Meanwhile, bring a large pot of salted water to a boil. Add the spaghetti and cook, stirring often to prevent the pasta from sticking together, until tender but still firm to the bite, about 10 minutes. Drain.

Add the spaghetti to the cream mixture and toss over medium-low heat until the chicken is heated through and the sauce coats the spaghetti thickly, about 4 minutes (do not boil). Season the pasta to taste with pepper.

Transfer the pasta to a large, wide serving bowl. Sprinkle with the walnuts and lemon zest, and serve.

polpette and spaghetti

4 SERVINGS

Polpette is the Italian word for meatballs, traditionally made with ground beef, veal, and pork. I get a lot of flack for putting ketchup in my meatballs, but nothing beats that tang!

1   SMALL ONION, GRATED

¼   CUP CHOPPED FRESH FLAT-LEAF PARSLEY

1   LARGE EGG

3   TABLESPOONS KETCHUP

3   GARLIC CLOVES, MINCED

1   TEASPOON SALT

¼   TEASPOON FRESHLY GROUND BLACK PEPPER

⅔   CUP FRESHLY GRATED PARMESAN CHEESE, PLUS MORE TO TASTE

¼   CUP DRIED ITALIAN-STYLE BREAD CRUMBS

6   OUNCES GROUND BEEF

6   OUNCES GROUND VEAL

6   OUNCES GROUND PORK

¼   CUP EXTRA-VIRGIN OLIVE OIL

5   CUPS MARINARA SAUCE (PAGE 144)

1   POUND SPAGHETTI

Whisk the onions, parsley, egg, ketchup, garlic, salt, and pepper together in a large bowl to blend. Stir in the ⅔ cup of Parmesan cheese and the bread crumbs, then mix in the beef, veal, and pork using your hands to combine everything gently but thoroughly. Shape the meat mixture into 1¼- to 1 ½-inch-diameter meatballs, using about 2 tablespoons for each.

Heat the oil in large, heavy frying pan over medium-high heat. Working in 2 batches, sauté the meatballs until browned on all sides, about 5 minutes. Use a slotted spoon to transfer the meatballs to a plate as they are browned. When all the meatballs are well browned, return them to the pan and add the marinara sauce. Simmer over medium-low heat until the sauce thickens slightly and the flavors blend, about 10 minutes. Season with salt and pepper.

Meanwhile, bring a large pot of salted water to a boil. Add the spaghetti and cook until tender but still firm to the bite, about 8 minutes. Drain.

Add the drained pasta to the frying pan with the sauce and meatballs, and toss gently to coat. Season the pasta to taste with salt and pepper. Transfer the pasta to a serving bowl. Sprinkle with additional Parmesan cheese, and serve.

rigatoni with steak

For most of the men in my family, there's nothing more satisfying than the combination of pasta and steak. So this is for all those meat-and-pasta lovers out there! It's also a smart way to make these pricy steaks go a bit further. I like to serve this with a full-bodied Chianti.

2	TABLESPOONS OLIVE OIL
2	(12-OUNCE) RIB-EYE STEAKS
	SALT AND FRESHLY GROUND BLACK PEPPER
2	ONIONS, THINLY SLICED
2	CARROTS, PEELED AND THINLY SLICED
4	GARLIC CLOVES, MINCED
½	TEASPOON DRIED OREGANO
¾	CUP DRY RED WINE
2	CUPS QUICK MARINARA SAUCE (PAGE 144)
1	CUP LOW-SODIUM BEEF BROTH
12	OUNCES DRIED RIGATONI
3	OUNCES SHAVED PARMESAN CHEESE

Heat the oil in a large, heavy frying pan over high heat. Sprinkle the steaks with salt and pepper. Cook the steaks until they are seared and brown but still rare in the center, about 3 minutes per side. Transfer the steaks to a plate and set aside to cool completely. Add the onions and carrots to the same pan and sauté over medium heat until the onions are translucent, about 8 minutes. Add the garlic and oregano, and sauté for 1 minute. Add the wine and simmer for 1 minute. Add the marinara sauce and broth. Cover and simmer over medium-low heat to allow the flavors to blend, about 10 minutes. Season the sauce to taste with salt and pepper.

Meanwhile, trim off any fat from the steaks, then cut the steaks into bite-size pieces and set aside. Bring a large pot of salted water to a boil. Add the rigatoni and cook, stirring often to prevent the pasta from sticking together, until it is tender but still firm to the bite, about 10 minutes. Drain.

Toss the rigatoni, reserved steak pieces, and any accumulated juices from the steaks with the sauce to coat. Transfer the pasta to bowls. Sprinkle with the Parmesan cheese and serve.

fusilli with shrimp and arugula

4 MAIN-COURSE SERVINGS OR 6 FIRST-COURSE SERVINGS

Shrimp and pasta are a wonderful pair that always looks and tastes a little bit fancy. This is a light, fresh pasta full of bright colors and flavors; it's perfect for a summer lunch.

¼ **CUP OLIVE OIL**

¼ **CUP FINELY CHOPPED SHALLOTS**

1 **TABLESPOON MINCED GARLIC**

¼ **TEASPOON CRUSHED DRIED RED PEPPER FLAKES**

1 **CUP DRY WHITE WINE**

1 **POUND LARGE SHRIMP, PEELED AND DEVEINED**

SALT

12 **OUNCES DRIED FUSILLI**

3 **CUPS (PACKED) ARUGULA, TORN INTO BITE-SIZE PIECES**

FRESHLY GROUND BLACK PEPPER

Heat the oil in a large, heavy skillet over medium heat. Add the shallots, garlic, and red pepper flakes; sauté until translucent, about 2 minutes. Add the wine. Simmer until the wine reduces by half, about 5 minutes. Add the shrimp and cook, stirring, just until they are pink, about 2 minutes.

Meanwhile, bring a large pot of salted water to a boil. Add the fusilli and cook, stirring often to prevent the pasta from sticking together, until tender but still firm to the bite, about 8 minutes. Drain.

Add the fusilli and arugula to the skillet with the shrimp. Toss to combine. Season the pasta to taste with salt and pepper. Transfer to a large bowl and serve.

quick marinara sauce

MAKES ABOUT 1½ QUARTS (6 CUPS)

Marinara sauce from the store is generally not bad, but it may contain flavorings and ingredients you don't want in your finished dish. This sauce is the bare-bones basic, flavored with fresh basil and dried oregano, then cooked briefly so it retains that bright, fresh flavor. When I make marinara sauce, I double the recipe and freeze it in 1- or 2-cup portions and then pull it out as needed.

2   (28-OUNCE) CANS WHOLE TOMATOES IN JUICE
1   BUNCH OF FRESH BASIL, STEMMED
½   CUP EXTRA-VIRGIN OLIVE OIL
2   SMALL ONIONS, FINELY CHOPPED
4   GARLIC CLOVES, FINELY CHOPPED
1   TEASPOON DRIED OREGANO
1   TEASPOON SUGAR
    SALT AND FRESHLY GROUND BLACK PEPPER

In a blender, purée the tomatoes with their juice and the basil until almost smooth. Set the tomato purée aside.

Heat the oil in a large, heavy saucepan over medium heat. Add the onions and garlic and sauté until very tender, about 12 minutes. Stir in the tomato purée, oregano, and sugar. Bring to a simmer over medium-high heat. Decrease the heat to medium and continue simmering until the sauce thickens slightly, stirring occasionally, about 10 minutes. Season the sauce to taste with salt and pepper. (The sauce can be made 1 day ahead. If storing for future use, cool, then cover and refrigerate. Rewarm over medium heat before using.)

ravioli with creamy tomato sauce

6 MAIN-COURSE SERVINGS

Frozen stuffed pastas are one of the best convenience foods available in today's grocery stores. I always have a few different shapes and flavors in my freezer for unexpected guests. Add a few of your own fresh ingredients and a quick marinara-based sauce like this one and you can make a gourmet meal in a flash.

SALT

1½ POUNDS FRESH OR FROZEN, THAWED SPINACH RAVIOLI OR TORTELLONI

2 TEASPOONS EXTRA-VIRGIN OLIVE OIL

1 CUP QUICK MARINARA SAUCE (PAGE 144)

½ CUP WHOLE-MILK RICOTTA CHEESE

FRESHLY GROUND BLACK PEPPER

3 TABLESPOONS FRESHLY GRATED PARMESAN CHEESE

2 TABLESPOONS THINLY SLICED FRESH BASIL

Bring a large pot of salted water to a boil. Add the ravioli and cook, stirring occasionally, until the pasta is tender but still firm to the bite, about 5 minutes. Drain, reserving ½ cup of the cooking water, and toss the ravioli with the oil in a large bowl to coat.

Meanwhile, bring the marinara sauce to a simmer in a medium, heavy saucepan over medium heat, whisking often. Whisk in the ricotta and enough reserved cooking water to thin the sauce to a desired consistency. Return the sauce to a simmer and season to taste with salt and pepper.

Spoon 3 tablespoons of sauce over the bottom of each of 6 bowls. Arrange the ravioli over the sauce, then drizzle the remaining sauce over the ravioli. Sprinkle with the Parmesan cheese, then the basil, and serve.

penne with sausage, artichokes, and sun-dried tomatoes

6 MAIN-COURSE SERVINGS

I love this pasta because it's fast, easy, yummy, and the colors make a beautiful presentation. It's also a very substantial dish, with the meat, veggies, and cheese all in one. The trick is to use frozen artichokes; they hold their shape in the sauce rather than becoming mush. Try this dish with whole wheat pasta, too; its hearty flavor holds its own with the sausage and other ingredients.

¾ CUP DRAINED OIL-PACKED SUN-DRIED TOMATOES, SLICED, 2 TABLESPOONS OF OIL RESERVED

1 POUND ITALIAN HOT SAUSAGES, CASINGS REMOVED

2 (8-OUNCE) PACKAGES FROZEN ARTICHOKE HEARTS, THAWED

2 LARGE GARLIC CLOVES, CHOPPED

1¾ CUPS REDUCED-SODIUM CHICKEN BROTH

½ CUP DRY WHITE WINE

SALT

12 OUNCES PENNE

½ CUP FRESHLY SHREDDED PARMESAN CHEESE, PLUS MORE FOR SERVING

⅓ CUP CHOPPED FRESH BASIL

¼ CUP CHOPPED FRESH FLAT-LEAF PARSLEY

8 OUNCES FRESH MOZZARELLA, DRAINED AND CUBED (OPTIONAL)

· FRESHLY GROUND BLACK PEPPER

Heat the oil reserved from the tomatoes in a large, heavy frying pan over a medium-high flame. Add the sausage and cook until brown, breaking up the meat into bite-size pieces with a fork, about 8 minutes. Transfer the sausage to a bowl. Add the artichokes and garlic to the same skillet, and sauté over medium heat until the garlic is tender, about 2 minutes. Add the broth, wine, and sun-dried tomatoes. Boil over medium-high heat, stirring occasionally, until the sauce reduces slightly, about 8 minutes.

Meanwhile, bring a large pot of salted water to a boil. Add the penne and cook, stirring often to prevent the pasta from sticking together, until tender but still firm to the bite, about 10 minutes. Drain the pasta (do not rinse). Add the pasta, sausage, ½ cup of the Parmesan cheese, the basil, and parsley to the artichoke mixture. Toss until the sauce is almost absorbed by the pasta. Stir in the mozzarella, if using. Season to taste with salt and pepper, and serve, passing additional Parmesan cheese alongside.

whole wheat spaghetti with swiss chard and pecorino cheese

4 MAIN-COURSE SERVINGS

When you're looking to lighten your pasta dishes, try whole wheat pasta. Its nutty, hearty, and delicious flavor blends perfectly with the herby flavor of the Swiss chard, and even a smaller portion will leave you feeling satisfied without the guilt.

2 **TABLESPOONS PINE NUTS**

1 **TABLESPOON EXTRA-VIRGIN OLIVE OIL**

2 **ONIONS, THINLY SLICED**

2 **BUNCHES OF SWISS CHARD, TRIMMED AND CHOPPED (ABOUT 14 CUPS)**

4 **GARLIC CLOVES, MINCED**

1 **(14½-OUNCE) CAN DICED TOMATOES IN JUICE**

¼ **CUP DRY WHITE WINE**

¼ **TEASPOON CRUSHED DRIED RED PEPPER FLAKES**

SALT AND FRESHLY GROUND BLACK PEPPER

8 **OUNCES WHOLE WHEAT SPAGHETTI**

¼ **CUP PITTED KALAMATA OLIVES, COARSELY CHOPPED**

2 **TABLESPOONS FRESHLY GRATED PECORINO CHEESE**

Preheat the oven to 300°F. Place the pine nuts on a heavy baking sheet or in a pie tin. Toast the nuts in the oven, stirring occasionally to ensure they brown evenly, until they are golden brown, about 10 minutes. (Alternatively, preheat a small, heavy skillet over a medium-low flame. Place the nuts in the hot skillet and stir them until they become golden brown, about 5 minutes.) Set the nuts aside.

Heat the oil in a large, heavy frying pan over medium-high heat. Add the onions and sauté until tender, about 8 minutes. Add the chard and sauté until it wilts, about 2 minutes. Add the garlic and sauté until fragrant, about 1 minute. Stir in the tomatoes with their juice, the wine, and the red pepper flakes. Bring to a boil. Decrease the heat to medium-low, cover, and simmer, stirring occasionally, until the tomatoes begin to break down and the chard is very tender, about 5 minutes. Season the chard mixture to taste with salt and pepper.

Meanwhile, bring a large pot of salted water to a boil. Add the spaghetti and cook, stirring often to prevent the pasta from sticking together, until tender but still firm to the bite, about 8 minutes. Drain. Add the spaghetti to the chard mixture and toss to combine.

Transfer the pasta to bowls; sprinkle the olives, cheese, and pine nuts on top and serve.

farfalle with asparagus and mushrooms

4 MAIN-COURSE SERVINGS OR 6 FIRST-COURSE SERVINGS

An incredibly simple pasta—you can do the entire prep and cooking in the time it takes for the water to boil and the pasta to cook. You could even omit the asparagus if it's not in season and add chopped parsley for a splash of color. It's the ultimate in everyday Italian cooking.

SALT

1 POUND DRIED FARFALLE

3 TABLESPOONS UNSALTED BUTTER

1 POUND CREMINI MUSHROOMS, TRIMMED AND THICKLY SLICED

1 POUND THIN ASPARAGUS, TRIMMED AND CUT CROSSWISE INTO 1-INCH PIECES

1 CUP MASCARPONE CHEESE

PINCH OF FRESHLY GRATED NUTMEG

¾ CUP TOASTED WALNUTS, COARSELY CHOPPED (SEE PAGE 221)

FRESHLY GROUND BLACK PEPPER

¼ CUP FRESHLY GRATED PARMESAN CHEESE

Bring a large pot of salted water to a boil. Add the farfalle and cook, stirring often to prevent the pasta from sticking together, until tender but still firm to the bite, about 12 minutes. Drain, reserving 1 cup of the cooking liquid.

Meanwhile, melt the butter in a large, heavy skillet over medium heat. Add the mushrooms and sauté until they are tender and most of their juices have evaporated, about 5 minutes. Add the asparagus and sauté until it is crisp-tender, about 5 minutes. Stir in the mascarpone and nutmeg. Add the farfalle and toss until the cheese coats the pasta, adding the reserved cooking liquid ¼ cup at a time to moisten. Stir in ½ cup of the walnuts. Season the pasta to taste with salt and pepper. Mound the pasta in a large, wide serving bowl. Sprinkle with the Parmesan cheese and remaining ¼ cup of walnuts, and serve.

red wine risotto with peas

Most risottos use white wine, but the red wine in this one makes it more elegant, romantic, and yummy. The wine tints the grains of rice a pale lilac that looks beautiful on a pale plate or bowl.

3½ CUPS REDUCED-SODIUM CHICKEN BROTH

3 TABLESPOONS UNSALTED BUTTER

1 CUP FINELY CHOPPED ONION

2 GARLIC CLOVES, MINCED

1 CUP ARBORIO RICE OR MEDIUM-GRAIN WHITE RICE

½ CUP DRY RED WINE

⅓ CUP FROZEN PEAS, DEFROSTED

¼ CUP CHOPPED FRESH FLAT-LEAF PARSLEY

½ CUP FRESHLY GRATED PARMESAN CHEESE, PLUS MORE FOR SERVING

SALT AND FRESHLY GROUND BLACK PEPPER

Bring the broth to a simmer over medium-high heat. Cover the broth and keep it warm over very low heat.

Melt the butter in a large, heavy saucepan over medium heat. Add the onion and sauté until translucent, about 8 minutes. Stir in the garlic and sauté for 30 seconds, until fragrant. Stir in the rice. Add the wine and stir until it is absorbed, about 1 minute. Add ¾ cup of the hot broth; simmer over medium-low heat, stirring often, until the liquid is absorbed, about 6 minutes. Repeat adding ¾ cup of hot broth 2 more times, stirring often, about 12 minutes longer. (At this point, the risotto can be set aside for up to 4 hours. Refrigerate the risotto—the rice will still be firm—and remaining broth, uncovered, until cool, then cover and keep them refrigerated.) Bring the remaining broth back to a simmer, then cover and keep it warm over very low heat before proceeding.

Stir ¾ cup of the hot broth into the partially cooked risotto over medium heat until the broth is absorbed and the risotto is hot, about 3 minutes. Add the remaining ½ cup of broth and simmer until the rice is just tender and the mixture is creamy, about 5 minutes longer. Stir in the peas and parsley. Mix in ½ cup of the Parmesan cheese. Season to taste with salt and pepper. Spoon the risotto into bowls. Sprinkle with additional cheese and serve.

dirty risotto

This has all the flavors that everyone loves most; it's cheesy, creamy, and smoky, with bits of bacon and sausage in every bite. Pure Italian comfort food.

- 5 **CUPS REDUCED-SODIUM CHICKEN BROTH**
- 2 **TABLESPOONS UNSALTED BUTTER**
- 2 **OUNCES PANCETTA, CHOPPED**
- 6 **OUNCES SPICY ITALIAN SAUSAGE, CASINGS REMOVED**
- ¾ **CUP FINELY CHOPPED ONION**
- 1 **CUP CHOPPED RED BELL PEPPER**
- 4 **OUNCES BUTTON MUSHROOMS, TRIMMED AND COARSELY CHOPPED**
- 1½ **CUPS ARBORIO RICE**
- ¾ **CUP DRY WHITE WINE**
- ½ **CUP FRESHLY GRATED PARMESAN CHEESE**
- ½ **TEASPOON SALT**
- ¼ **TEASPOON FRESHLY GROUND BLACK PEPPER**
- 1 **TABLESPOON CHOPPED FRESH FLAT-LEAF PARSLEY**

Bring the broth to a simmer in a medium saucepan. Cover the broth and keep hot over low heat.

In a large heavy saucepan, melt the butter over medium heat. Add the pancetta and sausage and sauté until golden brown, about 5 minutes. Add the onion, bell pepper, and mushrooms, and sauté until tender, about 8 minutes, scraping up the browned bits on the bottom of the pan. Add the rice and stir to coat with the oil. Add the wine and simmer until the wine has almost completely evaporated, about 1 minute. Add ½ cup of the simmering broth and stir until it is almost completely absorbed, about 2 minutes. Continue cooking the rice, adding the broth ½ cup at a time, stirring constantly and allowing each addition of broth to absorb before adding the next, until the rice is tender but still firm to the bite and the mixture is creamy, about 25 minutes total. Remove from the heat. Stir in the Parmesan cheese, salt, and pepper. Transfer the risotto to a serving bowl. Sprinkle with the parsley and serve immediately.

family-style
GET-TOGETHERS

These family-style recipes are designed to serve a crowd somewhat bigger than your everyday dinner gatherings; each will feed eight to ten people, and they can easily be adjusted for larger groups. But that doesn't mean these are formal, elaborate dishes; quite the contrary. The key here is not to worry too much about precise portion sizes. When I get together with good friends, everyone sits down as if they were gathered at a farmhouse table in Tuscany—like family—and helps themselves to as much or as little as they want. These stews, roasts, and vegetables require little preparation, and many of them can cook unattended. And that leaves you plenty of time for other things, like enjoying the company of your guests.

Good dessert ideas to round out these feasts would be the Raspberry Tiramisù (page 233) or the Zuccotto (page 239).

PIZZETTE WITH GORGONZOLA, TOMATO, AND BASIL

CROSTINI WITH GORGONZOLA, HONEY, AND WALNUTS

SUN-DRIED TOMATO AND MOZZARELLA KEBABS

SALAMI CRISPS WITH SOUR CREAM AND BASIL

TURKEY BOLOGNESE

BAKED ANGEL HAIR TIMBALE

FARMER'S PASTA

ZUPPA DI PESCE

VEAL STEW WITH CIPOLLINI ONIONS

POT ROAST WITH PORCINI MUSHROOMS

PANCETTA-WRAPPED PORK ROAST

VEGETABLE GRATIN

BAKED MASHED POTATOES WITH
PARMESAN CHEESE AND BREAD CRUMBS

pizzettes with gorgonzola, tomato, and basil

8 TO 10 SERVINGS

Pizzettes are bite-size pizzas, and you can top them with any of your favorite pizza toppings. This is a bit of a variation on the classic *margherita*—I find the gorgonzola and sweet cherry tomatoes make a great appetite enhancer. Other combos to try are grated fontina cheese, chopped mushrooms, and prosciutto, or coarse sea salt, extra-virgin olive oil, and fresh rosemary.

1 **BALL (12 OUNCES) PURCHASED PIZZA DOUGH**

5 **OUNCES GORGONZOLA CHEESE, CRUMBLED**

5 **OUNCES CHERRY TOMATOES, QUARTERED**

1 **TABLESPOON EXTRA-VIRGIN OLIVE OIL**

⅓ **CUP FRESH BASIL LEAVES, TORN INTO PIECES**

SALT AND FRESHLY GROUND BLACK PEPPER

Preheat the oven to 475°F. Roll out the pizza dough into a ¼-inch-thick round. Using a 2¼- to 2½-inch-diameter cookie cutter, cut out 30 dough circles. Arrange the circles on 2 large, heavy baking sheets. Sprinkle the Gorgonzola cheese over the circles. Top with the tomatoes, pressing them gently into the dough. Bake until the *pizzettes* are golden brown, about 10 minutes. Drizzle the *pizzettes* with the oil, then sprinkle with the basil, salt, and pepper. Arrange the *pizzettes* on a platter and serve immediately.

crostini with gorgonzola, honey, and walnuts

MAKES 24

What I love about this crostini recipe is that I can serve it as an appetizer before dinner, as an afternoon snack, or even as a dessert. It's a really interesting mixture of sweetness from the honey, salty-tang from the Gorgonzola, and crunchiness from the toasted baguette and walnuts.

2	TABLESPOONS OLIVE OIL
24	⅓-INCH-THICK DIAGONAL BAGUETTE SLICES
6	OUNCES CREAMY GORGONZOLA CHEESE, COARSELY CRUMBLED
⅔	CUP WALNUTS, TOASTED, COARSELY CHOPPED
1	RIPE FIG, THINLY SLICED CROSSWISE (OPTIONAL)
3	TABLESPOONS HONEY

Preheat the oven to 375°F. Arrange the baguette slices on a baking sheet in a single layer. Lightly brush the baguette slices with oil. Toast in the oven until the baguette slices are golden, about 8 minutes. (You can toast the baguette slices 1 day ahead. Cool, then store them at room temperature in an airtight container.)

Toss the Gorgonzola with the walnuts in a small bowl. Spoon the cheese mixture onto the baguette slices and press lightly to adhere. Return the baking sheet to the oven and bake until the cheese melts, about 8 minutes. Arrange the crostini on a platter. Top each with a slice of fig, if desired. Drizzle with honey and serve warm.

herb-coated goat cheese

MAKES 35

This fun way to serve goat cheese makes it look more festive and gives it more flavor. As a caterer I was always looking for new ways to serve everyone's favorite cheese and this became one of my most popular cocktail bites.

35 (½-INCH-THICK) SLICES OF BAGUETTE

3 TABLESPOONS OLIVE OIL

3 TABLESPOONS FINELY CHOPPED FRESH FLAT-LEAF PARSLEY

2½ TEASPOONS FINELY CHOPPED FRESH THYME LEAVES

2 TEASPOONS FINELY CHOPPED FRESH ROSEMARY

1 TEASPOON CHOPPED LEMON ZEST

1 TEASPOON COARSELY CRACKED BLACK PEPPER

¼ TEASPOON SALT

1 (11-OUNCE) LOG SOFT FRESH GOAT CHEESE

1½ TABLESPOONS EXTRA-VIRGIN OLIVE OIL OR MEYER LEMON OLIVE OIL (SEE PAGE 51)

FRESH HERB SPRIGS, FOR GARNISH

Preheat the oven to 375°F. Arrange the bread slices on two heavy large baking sheets. Brush the bread slices with olive oil and bake until the crostini are pale golden and crisp, about 15 minutes.

Meanwhile, stir the herbs, lemon zest, pepper, and salt together in a medium bowl to blend. Form the goat cheese into 1-inch-diameter balls, using about 2 teaspoons of cheese for each. Roll the cheese balls in the herb mixture to coat completely. Arrange the cheese balls on a platter. Drizzle the extra-virgin olive oil over and around the cheese balls. Serve with the crostini.

note: The crostini and cheese balls can be prepared 1 day ahead. Store the crostini in an airtight container at room temperature. Cover and refrigerate the cheese balls.

sun-dried tomato and mozzarella kebabs

8 TO 10 SERVINGS

This is a tricolor salad on a stick—perfect for large groups!

20 (8-INCH) WOODEN SKEWERS

20 OIL-PACKED SUN-DRIED TOMATOES, HALVED
     AND DRAINED, OIL RESERVED

40 MEDIUM FRESH BASIL LEAVES

40 SMALL FRESH WATER-PACKED MOZZARELLA BALLS, DRAINED
     SALT AND FRESHLY GROUND BLACK PEPPER

Onto 20 wooden skewers, alternately thread 1 sun-dried tomato half, 1 basil leaf, 1 mozzarella ball, 1 more basil leaf, 1 more sun-dried tomato half, and 1 more mozzarella ball. Arrange the skewers on a platter. Drizzle the reserved oil from the sun-dried tomatoes over the skewers. Sprinkle with salt and pepper, and serve.

salami crisps with sour cream and basil

MAKES 24 PIECES

Every time I make these for a party they absolutely disappear. If you like beef jerky you will *love* these. The recipe is easy to double or even triple for a big crowd and can be made ahead of time, too.

24 THIN SLICES ITALIAN DRY SALAMI (ABOUT 4 OUNCES)

⅓ CUP SOUR CREAM

3 TABLESPOONS THINLY SLICED FRESH BASIL LEAVES

Preheat the oven to 325°F. Line 2 heavy large baking sheets with aluminum foil. Arrange the salami in a single layer over the baking sheets. Bake until the salami slices are amber brown, watching closely to ensure they brown evenly, about 10 minutes. Transfer the salami crisps to a paper towel–lined baking sheet to absorb the excess oil. Set aside to cool. (The salami crisps can be made 8 hours ahead. Store at room temperature in an airtight container.)

Spoon a dollop of sour cream onto each salami crisp. Sprinkle with the basil and serve.

turkey bolognese

8 TO 10 SERVINGS

Of course Bolognese sauce is usually made with beef or other meats (and it cooks for quite a long time), but I love this quick, lighter variation. It's a great way to use up Thanksgiving turkey leftovers, especially since everyone seems to want white meat for sandwiches, leaving me all that rich, yummy thigh meat.

⅓   **CUP EXTRA-VIRGIN OLIVE OIL**

2   **ONIONS, CHOPPED**

6   **GARLIC CLOVES, MINCED**

2   **CELERY STALKS, FINELY CHOPPED**

1   **LARGE CARROT, PEELED AND FINELY CHOPPED**

1½   **POUNDS COARSELY SHREDDED COOKED TURKEY (PREFERABLY DARK MEAT)**

6   **CUPS QUICK MARINARA SAUCE (PAGE 144)**

1   **CUP WATER**

⅔   **CUP CHOPPED FRESH BASIL**

    SALT AND FRESHLY GROUND BLACK PEPPER

1½   **POUNDS SPAGHETTI**

    FRESHLY GRATED PARMESAN CHEESE

Heat the oil in a large, heavy pot over medium heat. Add the onions and garlic and sauté until translucent, about 8 minutes. Add the celery and carrot, and sauté until the vegetables are tender, about 8 minutes. Add the turkey and sauté 1 minute. Add the marinara sauce and water. Bring the sauce to a simmer over medium-high heat, then decrease the heat to medium-low and simmer gently for 25 minutes, stirring often, to allow the flavors to blend. Stir in the basil. Season the sauce generously to taste with salt and pepper. (The sauce can be made 1 week ahead. If storing for future use, cool the sauce completely, then transfer it to a container and freeze. Bring the sauce to a simmer before using.)

      Meanwhile, in a very large pot of boiling salted water, cook the spaghetti, stirring often to prevent the pasta from sticking together, until tender but still firm to the bite, about 8 minutes. Drain, reserving 1 cup of the cooking liquid. Add the pasta to the sauce and toss to coat, adding enough of the reserved cooking liquid to moisten as needed. Serve with the Parmesan.

baked angel hair timbale

This is my version of a dish that was served at my grandfather's store, DDL Foodshow, where it was always one of the biggest sellers. His had meatballs and a heavier bread dough, but I like to make mine with turkey sausage and a flaky puff pastry. It's still a filling dish, but just a bit more refined. This is the kind of dish that really wows your guests.

⅓ CUP PLUS ¼ CUP OLIVE OIL

6 JAPANESE EGGPLANTS (ABOUT 2 POUNDS TOTAL), CUT INTO 1-INCH CUBES

SALT AND FRESHLY GROUND BLACK PEPPER

1 TABLESPOON MINCED GARLIC

1 POUND TURKEY SAUSAGE, CASINGS REMOVED

⅓ CUP DRY RED WINE

3 CUPS QUICK MARINARA SAUCE (PAGE 144)

1 TEASPOON CRUSHED DRIED RED PEPPER FLAKES

8 OUNCES ANGEL HAIR PASTA

1 (17¼-OUNCE) PACKAGE FROZEN PUFF PASTRY (2 SHEETS), THAWED

1 POUND MOZZARELLA CHEESE, DICED

1 CUP FRESHLY GRATED PARMESAN CHEESE

Heat ⅓ cup of the oil in a large frying pan over medium-high heat. Add half of the eggplant cubes and toss to coat in the oil. Sprinkle with salt and pepper. Sauté the eggplant until it is golden and tender, about 10 minutes. Decrease the heat to medium.

Add half of the garlic and sauté until it is tender, about 2 minutes longer. Using a slotted spoon, transfer the eggplant mixture to a large bowl. Repeat with the remaining ¼ cup of oil and the remaining eggplant and garlic. Add to the bowl with the first batch.

Add the sausage and wine to the same frying pan. Cook over medium-high heat until the wine evaporates and the sausage is brown, breaking the sausage into pieces with the back of the spoon, about 8 minutes. Add the sausage, marinara sauce, and red pepper flakes to the bowl with the eggplant mixture, and toss to combine.

Meanwhile, bring a large pot of salted water to a boil over high heat. Add the angel hair and cook for 1 minute, stirring constantly. Drain. Toss the angel hair with the eggplant mixture. Cool completely.

Preheat the oven to 375°F. Roll out 1 pastry sheet on a floured surface to a 13½-inch square. Transfer to a 9-inch springform pan, allowing the excess pastry to hang over the rim.

Add the mozzarella and Parmesan cheeses to the cooled eggplant and sausage, and toss to combine. Spoon the mixture into the pan. Roll out the second pastry sheet to a 13-inch square. Place the pastry over the pasta filling. Pinch the edges of the pastry sheets together to seal. Trim the overhanging pastry edges to about 1 inch. Fold the pastry edges in to form a decorative border. Cut a slit in the center of the top crust to allow steam to escape.

Bake until the pastry is brown and puffed on top, about 1 hour and 30 minutes. Let stand for 20 minutes. Remove the pan sides and serve.

farmer's pasta

This is called Farmer's Pasta because it's a substantial dish that was a favorite of farmers who worked outdoors all day and wanted hearty comfort food when they came in to eat. This dish is all about the different cheeses—mild mozzarella, gooey and floral fontina, the salty yet buttery Parmesan, and sharp and tangy Provolone. Sure it's rich, but hey, it's a feast, right? Indulge yourself and your guests!

- **BUTTER, FOR BAKING DISH**
- 2 **TABLESPOONS OLIVE OIL**
- 6 **OUNCES SLICED PANCETTA OR BACON, CHOPPED**
- 4 **TEASPOONS MINCED GARLIC**
- 3 **TABLESPOONS ALL-PURPOSE FLOUR**
- 4 **CUPS WHOLE MILK**
- 3 **CUPS HEAVY CREAM**
- 8 **OUNCES FONTINA CHEESE, GRATED**
- 6 **OUNCES MOZZARELLA CHEESE, GRATED**
- ¾ **CUP FRESHLY GRATED PARMESAN CHEESE**
- **SALT**
- 1 **POUND PENNE PASTA**
- 3 **TABLESPOONS CHOPPED FRESH FLAT-LEAF PARSLEY**
- 3 **TABLESPOONS CHOPPED FRESH BASIL**
- 6 **OUNCES PROVOLONE CHEESE, CUBED**
- **FRESHLY GROUND BLACK PEPPER**
- 2 **CUPS COARSE FRESH BREAD CRUMBS**

Preheat the oven to 375°F. Butter a 13 × 9 × 2-inch baking dish. Heat 1 tablespoon of the oil in a large, heavy saucepan over medium-high heat. Add the pancetta and sauté until golden and crisp, about 5 minutes. Using a slotted spoon, transfer the pancetta to a small bowl. Reduce the heat to medium. Add 3 teaspoons of the garlic and sauté until fragrant, about 30 seconds. Add the flour and whisk for 2 minutes. Whisk in the milk and cream. Bring to a boil over medium-high heat, then reduce the heat to medium and simmer, whisking often, until the sauce thickens slightly, about 5 minutes. Whisk in all the fontina, mozzarella, and Parmesan cheeses.

Meanwhile, bring a large pot of salted water to a boil. Add the penne and cook, stirring occasionally to prevent the pasta from sticking together, until al dente, about 8 minutes. Drain and transfer to a large bowl. Pour the cheese sauce over the penne. Add the parsley and basil, and toss to coat. Let it stand until the mixture cools and the sauce thickens slightly, tossing occasionally, about 10 minutes. Stir in the Provolone cheese and the crispy pancetta. Season the pasta mixture to taste with salt and pepper. Transfer the pasta mixture to the prepared dish.

Heat the remaining 1 tablespoon of oil in a large, heavy skillet over medium heat. Add the remaining teaspoon of garlic and sauté until fragrant, about 30 seconds. Remove from the heat. Add the bread crumbs and toss to coat. Sprinkle the bread crumb mixture over the pasta mixture.

Bake, uncovered, until the sauce bubbles and the bread crumbs are golden brown, about 20 minutes.

zuppa di pesce

{FISH SOUP}

6 SERVINGS

I know this recipe has a long list of ingredients, but once you have everything assembled, the cooking time required is actually very minimal. And the rich flavors that the shellfish contribute to the savory broth are second to none. If you're really pressed for time, you can skip the toasts and aïoli, but the garlicky mayo really gives the broth body and zest.

- 1 **BAY LEAF**
- 1 **LARGE FRESH ROSEMARY SPRIG**
- 1 **TABLESPOON FENNEL SEEDS, COARSELY CRUSHED**
- 3 **TABLESPOONS OLIVE OIL**
- 1 **FENNEL BULB, CHOPPED**
- 3 **LARGE SHALLOTS, CHOPPED**
- 1 **(28-OUNCE) CAN DICED TOMATOES IN JUICE**
- 1¼ **CUPS DRY WHITE WINE**
- 3 **CUPS FISH BROTH, BOTTLED CLAM JUICE, OR VEGETABLE BROTH**
- ¼ **CUP TOMATO PASTE**
- 8 **SMALL LITTLENECK CLAMS, SCRUBBED**
- 1 **POUND MUSSELS, SCRUBBED AND DEBEARDED**
- 8 **OUNCES RUSSET POTATOES, PEELED AND CUT INTO ¾-INCH CUBES**
- 1½ **POUNDS ASSORTED FIRM-FLESHED FISH FILLETS, SUCH AS HALIBUT, SALMON, OR TUNA, CUT INTO 2-INCH CHUNKS**
- 1 **POUND UNCOOKED LARGE SHRIMP, PEELED AND DEVEINED**
- 2 **EARS OF CORN, HUSKED AND QUARTERED CROSSWISE**
- 2 **TABLESPOONS CHOPPED FRESH FLAT-LEAF PARSLEY**
   SALT AND FRESHLY GROUND BLACK PEPPER
   GARLIC TOASTS WITH RED PEPPER AÏOLI (RECIPE FOLLOWS)

Put the bay leaf, rosemary, and fennel seeds in a cheesecloth bag. Set the sachet aside. Heat the oil in a very large pot over medium heat. Add the chopped fennel and shallots, and sauté until the fennel is tender, about 6 minutes. Add the tomatoes with their juice, the wine, and the fish broth. Stir in the tomato paste. Add the herb sachet and bring the liquid to a boil. Reduce the heat to medium-low. Cover and simmer until the flavors blend, about 10 minutes.

Add the clams to the cooking liquid. Cover and cook until the clams open, about 10 minutes (discard any clams that do not open). Using tongs, transfer the clams to a bowl. Repeat using the mussels. Add the potatoes to the cooking liquid and simmer until they are almost tender, about 10 minutes. Add the fish, shrimp, and corn. Simmer until the fish and shrimp are just cooked, and the corn is heated through, about 5 minutes. Return the clams and mussels to the soup. Discard the bay leaf and stir in the parsley. Season the soup to taste with salt and pepper.

Ladle the soup into bowls and serve with the garlic toasts with red pepper aïoli.

garlic toasts with red pepper aïoli

aïoli

2 GARLIC CLOVES

½ CUP ROASTED RED BELL PEPPERS, DRAINED AND PATTED DRY

⅓ CUP MAYONNAISE

2 TABLESPOONS OLIVE OIL

SALT AND FRESHLY GROUND BLACK PEPPER

toasts

12 (½-INCH-THICK) SLICES CIABATTA OR OTHER COUNTRY-STYLE WHITE BREAD

2 TABLESPOONS OLIVE OIL

SALT AND FRESHLY GROUND BLACK PEPPER

2 GARLIC CLOVES, HALVED

aïoli

Finely chop the garlic in a food processor. Add the peppers and blend until almost smooth. Blend in the mayonnaise. With the machine running, blend in the oil. Season the aïoli to taste with salt and pepper. Transfer the aïoli to a small bowl. (The aïoli can be made 2 days ahead. Cover and refrigerate.)

toasts

Preheat the oven to 400°F. Brush the bread slices with the oil. Arrange the bread on a baking sheet and sprinkle with salt and pepper. Bake until the bread is crisp and golden, about 5 minutes. Immediately rub the garlic clove halves over the hot toasts.

Spread with some of the aïoli and serve.

veal stew with cipollini onions

8 TO 10 SERVINGS

When you're entertaining a bunch of friends, there's nothing better than a stew. It's comforting, soothing, and yummy. This one is especially appealing because it's virtually a one-pot meal, with lots of vegetables and a delicious sauce to dunk bread into. What could be easier? Feel free to substitute lamb, beef, or chicken for the veal.

28 **CIPOLLINI ONIONS**

4 **TABLESPOONS OLIVE OIL**

5 **POUNDS VEAL STEW MEAT**

SALT AND FRESHLY GROUND BLACK PEPPER

⅓ **CUP ALL-PURPOSE FLOUR**

6 **GARLIC CLOVES, FINELY CHOPPED**

1 **TABLESPOON CHOPPED FRESH THYME**

2½ **CUPS DRY WHITE WINE**

5 **CUPS REDUCED-SODIUM CHICKEN BROTH**

1 **(14½-OUNCE) CAN DICED TOMATOES IN JUICE**

28 **SMALL RED-SKINNED POTATOES, HALVED**

2 **LARGE CARROTS, PEELED AND CUT INTO 1-INCH PIECES**

¼ **CUP CHOPPED FRESH FLAT-LEAF PARSLEY**

In a large saucepan of boiling water, cook the unpeeled onions for 2 minutes. Drain and cool. Peel the onions and cut off the root ends.

Meanwhile, heat 2 tablespoons of the oil in a very large, heavy pot or casserole over medium-high heat. Sprinkle the veal with salt and pepper. Toss the veal with the flour in a large bowl to coat. Working in 3 batches, add the veal to the pot and cook until browned, adding another tablespoon of oil as needed, about 10 minutes per batch. Using a slotted spoon, transfer the browned veal to a bowl. Add the garlic and thyme to the same pot and sauté over medium heat until tender and fragrant, about 30 seconds. Add the wine and simmer over medium-high heat until reduced by half, stirring to scrape up the browned bits on the bottom of the pot, about 5 minutes. Return the veal to the pot.

Stir in the broth and tomatoes with their juice. Cover partially and simmer over medium-low heat for 15 minutes. Add the onions, potatoes, and carrots to the stew and simmer uncovered until the veal and vegetables are tender and the juices thicken, stirring occasionally, about 45 minutes. Stir in the parsley. Season the stew to taste with salt and pepper. Ladle the stew into bowls and serve.

pot roast with porcini mushrooms

{STRACOTTO}

8 TO 10 SERVINGS

Stracotto literally means "overcooked." The beautiful ease of a pot roast is that once you've added all the ingredients, you can walk away and forget about it for several hours. This kind of cooking technique, known as braising, delivers moist, tender meat every time and succulent pan juices that are delicious over polenta or any kind of potatoes.

1   (5-POUND) BONELESS BEEF CHUCK ROAST

    SALT AND FRESHLY GROUND BLACK PEPPER

2   TABLESPOONS OLIVE OIL

2   ONIONS, CHOPPED

6   GARLIC CLOVES, COARSELY CHOPPED

1   CUP DRY RED WINE

1¾ CUPS CANNED LOW-SODIUM BEEF BROTH

½   OUNCE DRIED PORCINI MUSHROOMS

1   LARGE SPRIG OF FRESH ROSEMARY

Preheat the oven to 350°F. Pat the beef dry with paper towels and sprinkle generously with salt and pepper. Heat the oil in a heavy, 6-quart pot or Dutch oven over medium-high heat. Add the beef and cook until browned on all sides, about 12 minutes. (Don't rush this step, which is what creates the deep rich flavor in the finished dish.) Transfer the beef to a bowl.

Reduce the heat to medium. Add the onions to the same pan and sauté until tender, scraping up the brown bits on the bottom of the pot, about 5 minutes. Add the garlic and sauté for 1 minute. Add the wine and boil for 1 minute. Stir in the broth and mushrooms. Return the beef to the pan and bring the liquids to a boil. Cover the pot and transfer to the oven. Braise until the beef is fork-tender, about 3 hours, turning the beef over halfway through.

Transfer the beef to a cutting board. Tent with foil and let stand for 15 minutes. Meanwhile, spoon any excess fat off the top of the pan juices. Transfer the pan juices and vegetables to a blender and purée until smooth. In a medium, heavy saucepan, combine the sauce and rosemary sprig. Bring to a boil, then season the sauce to taste with salt and pepper.

Cut the beef across the grain into ½-inch-thick slices. Arrange the sliced beef on a platter. Spoon some of the sauce over and serve, passing the remaining sauce in a gravy boat.

pancetta-wrapped pork roast

8 TO 10 SERVINGS

When I'm cooking for a crowd, I love to make large roasts like this one—the preparation is the same whether I'm serving six or sixteen (this can be easily doubled), and all the work is done in advance. Plus, the smell of the meat roasting in the oven when guests arrive is just fantastic. The pancetta keeps the meat moist and with the herby rub the pork is simply delicious.

- 10 LARGE GARLIC CLOVES
- 1½ TABLESPOONS FINELY CHOPPED FRESH THYME
- 1 TABLESPOON FINELY CHOPPED FRESH ROSEMARY
- 1 TABLESPOON OLIVE OIL
- 1 (4½- TO 5-POUND) TIED BONELESS PORK LOIN ROAST
  SALT AND FRESHLY GROUND BLACK PEPPER
- 6 OUNCES THINLY SLICED PANCETTA OR BACON
- 2 CUPS REDUCED-SODIUM CHICKEN BROTH
- 2 CUPS DRY WHITE WINE

In a small food processor, blend the garlic, thyme, rosemary, and oil, scraping down the sides of the bowl occasionally, until the garlic is minced.

Untie the pork roast to separate the 2 pork loins. Sprinkle the pork generously with salt and pepper. Arrange the pancetta slices on a work surface, overlapping slightly to form a rectangle. Spread a fourth of the garlic mixture over the flat side of one pork loin, then top with the remaining pork loin, flat side down, to reform the pork roast. Using kitchen twine, tie the pork roast to secure the loins in place. Spread the remaining garlic mixture over the surface of the pork and place it on top of the pancetta. Wrap the pancetta slices around the pork to cover as completely as possible. Place the pork in a roasting pan. Cover and refrigerate for at least 1 hour and up to 24 hours.

Preheat the oven to 450°F. Pour ¾ cup of the broth and ¾ cup of the wine into the roasting pan. Roast the pork, adding more broth and wine to the pan juices every 20 minutes, until a meat thermometer inserted into the center registers 135°F for medium-rare, about 1 hour and 15 minutes. Transfer the pork to a cutting board. Tent with aluminum foil and let stand for 10 minutes. Pour the pan drippings into a glass measuring cup and spoon off any fat that rises to the top.

Using a large sharp carving knife, cut the pork into ¼-inch-thick slices, then serve with the pan juices.

vegetable gratin

This will get your guests to eat their vegetables. Douse any vegetable with cheese and cream, top it with crumbs, and bake it in the oven—who could refuse that?

3	TABLESPOONS UNSALTED BUTTER
	SALT
1	HEAD OF CAULIFLOWER (ABOUT 2¼ POUNDS), CUT INTO LARGE FLORETS
5	LARGE STALKS OF BROCCOLI (ABOUT 2 POUNDS), CUT INTO 2-INCH FLORETS
2	TABLESPOONS ALL-PURPOSE FLOUR
1¼	CUPS HEAVY CREAM
1¼	CUPS WHOLE MILK
3	OUNCES FONTINA CHEESE, SHREDDED
3	OUNCES PROVOLONE CHEESE, SHREDDED
½	CUP PLUS 2 TABLESPOONS GRATED PECORINO ROMANO CHEESE
	FRESHLY GROUND BLACK PEPPER
2	TABLESPOONS DRIED ITALIAN-STYLE SEASONED BREAD CRUMBS

Preheat the oven to 500°F. Grease a 13 × 9 × 2-inch baking dish with 1 tablespoon of the butter. Bring a large pot of salted water to a boil over high heat. Add the cauliflower florets and cook for 2 minutes. Using a slotted spoon, transfer the cauliflower to the prepared dish. Repeat with the broccoli.

Meanwhile, melt the remaining 2 tablespoons of butter in a medium, heavy saucepan over medium heat. Add the flour and whisk for 1 minute. Whisk in the cream and milk. Bring to a boil over medium-high heat. Decrease the heat to medium and simmer until the sauce thickens slightly, whisking often, about 2 minutes. Remove the saucepan from the heat. Add the fontina cheese, Provolone cheese, and ½ cup of the Pecorino Romano. Stir until the cheeses have melted. Season the sauce with salt and pepper. Pour the sauce over the vegetables and toss to coat.

In a small bowl, stir the bread crumbs and remaining 2 tablespoons of Pecorino cheese together. Sprinkle over the gratin. Bake uncovered until the topping is golden brown and the sauce is bubbly, about 20 minutes.

baked mashed potatoes with parmesan cheese and bread crumbs

6 TO 8 SERVINGS

This is my aunt's holiday mashed potato casserole. My favorite part is the crispy crust on top. It's another great make-ahead dish that can go into the oven right when you take the turkey out; it will heat while you make the gravy and carve the bird.

- 1 **TABLESPOON UNSALTED BUTTER, PLUS ½ CUP (1 STICK) UNSALTED BUTTER, MELTED**
  SALT
- 4 **POUNDS RUSSET POTATOES, PEELED AND CUT INTO 1-INCH PIECES**
- 1 **CUP WHOLE MILK, AT ROOM TEMPERATURE**
- 1½ **CUPS SHREDDED MOZZARELLA CHEESE**
- 1 **CUP FRESHLY GRATED PARMESAN CHEESE**
  FRESHLY GROUND BLACK PEPPER
- 2 **TABLESPOONS DRIED PLAIN BREAD CRUMBS**

Preheat the oven to 400°F. Coat a 13 × 9 × 2 inch baking dish with the 1 tablespoon of butter. Bring a large pot of salted water to a boil and cook the potatoes until they are very tender, about 15 minutes. Drain; return the potatoes to the same pot and mash well. Beat in the milk and melted butter, then mix in the mozzarella cheese and ¾ cup of the Parmesan cheese. Season to taste with salt and pepper. Transfer the potatoes to the prepared baking dish. In a small bowl, stir together the bread crumbs and remaining ¼ cup of Parmesan cheese. Sprinkle the bread crumb mixture over the mashed potatoes. (The dish can be prepared to this point up to 6 hours ahead. Cover and chill. Bring back to room temperature before baking.)

Bake uncovered until the topping is golden brown, about 20 minutes.

FAMILY FEASTS

In my family a holiday is a reason to make
delicacies we don't eat any other time of the year. From seafood on
Christmas to sweet ricotta cheese pie on Easter, these are very personal
dishes for me that evoke wonderful memories of boisterous gatherings
with three generations present. And since my family has been in America more than twenty years, Thanksgiving is a big deal for us, too. Of
course, we give our turkey day an Italian flair. These are some of my
favorite special dishes for special occasions.

Christmas is the only time of year that my whole family gets
together. All thirty of us congregate at my grandfather's house and sit
at a rectangular table eating until our tummies burst. My grandfather
always plays Santa and hands out all the gifts under the tree.

BELLINI BAR

LIMONCELLO SPRITZERS

ROSÉ WINE WITH FRESH SAGE AND LEMON

TURKEY WITH HERBES DE PROVENCE AND CITRUS

CIABATTA STUFFING WITH CHESTNUTS AND PANCETTA

BUTTERNUT SQUASH LASAGNA

INSALATA DI RINFORZO

HOLIDAY SALAD

EASTER PIE

PIZZA RUSTICA

EASTER LAMB

ROASTED RED SNAPPER WITH PARSLEY VINAIGRETTE

LINGUINE WITH SPICY RED CLAM SAUCE

PANETTONE BREAD PUDDING WITH AMARETTO SAUCE

bellini bar

When I want to create a festive holiday feel, I assemble a make-your-own bellini bar. The original bellini was made with peach nectar, but now the definition of this classic apéritif has expanded to include many other flavors. These are some that my family and I really enjoy.

- 2 CUPS SUGAR
- 1 CUP WATER
- 1 (16-OUNCE) BAG FROZEN PEACHES, THAWED
- 1 TEASPOON GRATED ORANGE ZEST
- 1 (16-OUNCE) BAG FROZEN STRAWBERRIES, THAWED
- 1 (16-OUNCE) BAG FROZEN BLUEBERRIES OR BLACKBERRIES, THAWED
- 4 TO 6 (750-ML) BOTTLES PROSECCO OR OTHER SPARKLING WINE, CHILLED
  FRESH STRAWBERRIES, RASPBERRIES, AND BLUEBERRIES, FOR GARNISH
  ORANGE PEEL TWISTS, FOR GARNISH

Stir the sugar and water in a large saucepan over medium heat until the sugar dissolves, about 5 minutes. Cool completely. (The sugar syrup can be made up to a week in advance and stored in the refrigerator.)

Purée the peaches and orange zest in a blender with ½ cup of the sugar syrup until smooth; strain through a fine-mesh strainer into a bowl. Purée the strawberries in a clean blender with ⅓ cup of the sugar syrup until smooth; strain through a clean fine-mesh strainer into another bowl. Discard the seeds. Purée the blueberries in a clean blender with ⅓ cup of the sugar syrup until smooth; strain through a clean fine-mesh strainer into a third bowl. Discard the seeds and solids. (The fruit purées can be made 1 day ahead. Cover separately and refrigerate.)

Pour each of the purées into clear glass bowls or small pitchers. For each serving, pour 2 to 4 tablespoons of the desired fruit purée into a champagne flute. Slowly pour enough Prosecco into the flute to fill. Gently stir to blend. Garnish with a piece or two of fresh fruit or an orange peel twist and serve.

limoncello spritzers

6 SERVINGS

This is a bubbly and festive drink to start off a holiday meal or party.

CRUSHED ICE
3 **CUPS LIMONCELLO (RECIPE FOLLOWS)**
12 **TABLESPOONS FRESH LEMON JUICE**
1½ **CUPS CLUB SODA**

Fill 6 tumblers halfway with the ice. Stir ½ cup of the *limoncello* and 2 tablespoons of the lemon juice into each glass. Top with ¼ cup of club soda and serve.

limoncello

MAKES 7 CUPS

Limoncello is a liqueur made from fermented lemon peel. It's light and refreshing and usually sipped at the end of a meal as a digestive. The best *limoncello* comes from the island of Capri and the Amalfi coast of Italy.

10 **LEMONS**
1 **(750-ML) BOTTLE VODKA**
3½ **CUPS WATER**
2½ **CUPS SUGAR**

Using a vegetable peeler, remove the peel from the lemons in long strips (reserve the lemons for another use). Using a small sharp knife, trim away the white pith from the lemon peels; discard the pith. Place the lemon peels in a 2-quart pitcher. Pour the vodka over the peels. Cover and steep the lemon peels in the vodka for 4 days at room temperature.

Stir the water and sugar in a large saucepan over medium heat until the sugar dissolves, about 5 minutes. Cool completely. Pour the sugar syrup into the vodka mixture. Cover and let stand at room temperature overnight. Strain the *limoncello* through a mesh strainer. Discard the peels. Transfer the *limoncello* to bottles. Seal the bottles and refrigerate until cold, at least 4 hours and up to 1 month.

rosé wine with fresh sage and lemon

MAKES ABOUT 3 CUPS

I make this wine during the holidays and give it away as gifts in decorative glass bottles that I buy at the craft shop. Serve it as an apértif before meals.

1 (750-ML) BOTTLE ROSÉ WINE

8 FRESH SAGE LEAVES, BRUISED

PEEL OF 1 LEMON REMOVED IN LONG STRIPS WITH A VEGETABLE PEELER

Combine the wine, sage, and lemon peel in a clear glass container. Cover and let stand at room temperature for 1 day. Strain the wine into a pitcher and discard the solids. Cover the wine and refrigerate it for up to 2 weeks. I prefer to serve it at room temperature but you can also serve it chilled.

turkey with herbes de provence and citrus

8 TO 10 SERVINGS

My Italian twist on Thanksgiving. Most birds are very dry and tasteless, but the citrus and herbs in the cavity of the bird really do penetrate the meat and give this turkey a fabulous fresh aroma and moistness.

1 (14- TO 15-POUND) TURKEY, NECK AND GIBLETS RESERVED

1 ORANGE, CUT INTO WEDGES

1 LEMON, CUT INTO WEDGES

1 ONION, CUT INTO WEDGES

6 FRESH ROSEMARY SPRIGS

6 FRESH SAGE SPRIGS

6 FRESH OREGANO SPRIGS

7 TABLESPOONS UNSALTED BUTTER

2 TABLESPOONS HERBES DE PROVENCE

1 TABLESPOON OLIVE OIL

1½ TEASPOONS SALT, PLUS MORE TO TASTE

1½ TEASPOONS FRESHLY GROUND BLACK PEPPER, PLUS MORE TO TASTE

6 CUPS (ABOUT) CANNED REDUCED-SODIUM CHICKEN BROTH

⅓ CUP ALL-PURPOSE FLOUR

to make the turkey

Position the rack in the lowest third of the oven and preheat the oven to 400°F. Rinse the turkey and pat it dry with paper towels. Place the turkey on a rack set inside a large roasting pan. Stuff the orange and lemon wedges, onion, and 2 sprigs of each fresh herb into the main turkey cavity. Using kitchen twine, tie the legs together to hold the shape of the turkey. In a small saucepan, stir 2 tablespoons of the butter, the herbes de Provence, oil, and 1½ teaspoons each of the salt and pepper over medium heat just until the butter melts. Rub the butter mixture all over the turkey and between the turkey breast meat and skin. Place the turkey neck and giblets in the roasting pan. (The turkey can be prepared 1 day ahead. Cover and refrigerate. Let stand at room temperature for 30 minutes before roasting.)

(recipe continues)

Cover the turkey breast with foil. Roast for 20 minutes. Pour 3 cups of the broth into the pan and stir to scrape up any brown bits on the bottom of the pan around the turkey. Add the remaining sprigs of fresh herbs to the pan juices. Return the pan to the oven and roast the turkey for 40 minutes. Reduce the oven temperature to 350°F and discard the foil. Pour 1 cup of broth into the pan. Continue roasting the turkey, basting occasionally with pan juices, until an instant-read meat thermometer inserted into the thickest part of the thigh registers 160°F, or until the juices run clear when the thickest part of the thigh is pierced with a skewer, about 1 hour 30 minutes longer. Transfer the turkey to a platter and tent with foil. Let stand for 30 minutes while you prepare the gravy.

to make the gravy

Strain the turkey pan juices through a sieve and into a 4-cup glass measuring cup; discard the solids. Spoon off the fat that rises to the top of the pan juices. Add enough chicken broth to the pan juices to measure 4 cups total. Melt the remaining 5 tablespoons butter in a large, heavy saucepan over medium-high heat. Add the flour and whisk for 1 minute. Gradually whisk in the pan juices. Simmer until the gravy thickens slightly, whisking often, about 10 minutes. Season with salt and pepper. Serve the turkey with the gravy.

ciabatta stuffing with chestnuts and pancetta

Stuffing is one of my favorite dishes at Thanksgiving and this is how I've Italianized it. My aunts always used to stuff chickens with chestnuts, pancetta, and Parmesan, and I think it works perfectly with the Thanksgiving menu. I always cook stuffing in a separate dish because it has a better texture that way and doesn't draw the juices out of the meat.

- 6 TABLESPOONS (¾ STICK) UNSALTED BUTTER, PLUS MORE FOR BAKING DISH
- 8 OUNCES THINLY SLICED PANCETTA OR BACON, CUT INTO ¼-INCH DICE
- 2 LARGE ONIONS, FINELY CHOPPED
- 2 CARROTS, PEELED AND FINELY CHOPPED
- 3 CELERY STALKS, FINELY CHOPPED
- 2 TABLESPOONS CHOPPED FRESH ROSEMARY
- 3 GARLIC CLOVES, CHOPPED
- 2 (7.4-OUNCE) JARS ROASTED PEELED WHOLE CHESTNUTS, COARSELY BROKEN
- 1 POUND DAY-OLD CIABATTA OR OTHER COUNTRY-STYLE WHITE BREAD, CUT INTO ¾-INCH CUBES (ABOUT 12 CUPS)
- ⅔ CUP FRESHLY GRATED PARMESAN CHEESE
- ¼ CUP CHOPPED FRESH FLAT-LEAF PARSLEY
- 1 CUP CANNED REDUCED-SODIUM CHICKEN BROTH, OR MORE AS NEEDED
   SALT AND FRESHLY GROUND BLACK PEPPER
- 2 LARGE EGGS, BEATEN TO BLEND

Preheat the oven to 350°F. Butter a 15 × 10 × 2-inch glass baking dish. Melt 2 tablespoons of the butter in a large, heavy skillet over medium heat. Add the pancetta and sauté until crisp and golden, about 10 minutes. Using a slotted spoon, transfer the pancetta to a large bowl. Melt the remaining 4 tablespoons of butter in the same skillet over medium-high heat. Add the onions, carrots, celery, rosemary, and garlic. Sauté until the onions are very tender, about 12 minutes. Gently stir in the chestnuts. Transfer the onion mixture to the large bowl with the pancetta. Add the bread, Parmesan cheese, and parsley, and toss to coat. Add enough broth to the stuffing mixture to moisten. Season the stuffing to taste with salt and pepper. Mix in the eggs.

Transfer the stuffing to the prepared dish. Cover with buttered foil, buttered side down, and bake until the stuffing is heated through, about 30 minutes. Uncover and continue baking until the top is crisp and golden, about 15 minutes longer.

butternut squash lasagna

At Thanksgiving, pumpkin is expected to make an appearance on the holiday table, but I'm not that big on pumpkin so I substitute butternut squash and serve it with the entrée instead of for dessert. It tastes better and is available all year long, so I can make this anytime. Don't be put off by the amaretti cookies; they're the secret ingredient.

- 1 **TABLESPOON OLIVE OIL**
- 1 **(1½- TO 2-POUND) BUTTERNUT SQUASH, PEELED, SEEDED, AND CUT INTO 1-INCH CUBES**
- **SALT AND FRESHLY GROUND BLACK PEPPER**
- ½ **CUP WATER**
- 3 **AMARETTI COOKIES, CRUMBLED**
- ¼ **CUP (½ STICK) UNSALTED BUTTER, PLUS MORE FOR BAKING DISH**
- ¼ **CUP ALL-PURPOSE FLOUR**
- 3½ **CUPS WHOLE MILK**
- **PINCH OF NUTMEG**
- ¾ **CUP LIGHTLY PACKED FRESH BASIL LEAVES**
- 12 **NO-BOIL LASAGNA NOODLES (SEE NOTE)**
- 2½ **CUPS SHREDDED WHOLE-MILK MOZZARELLA CHEESE**
- ⅓ **CUP FRESHLY GRATED PARMESAN CHEESE**

Heat the oil in a large, heavy skillet over medium-high heat. Add the squash and toss to coat. Sprinkle with salt and pepper. Pour the water into the skillet, then cover and simmer over medium heat, stirring occasionally, until the squash is tender, about 20 minutes. Cool slightly, then transfer the squash to a food processor. Add the amaretti cookies and blend until smooth. Season the squash purée to taste with more salt and pepper.

Melt the ¼ cup butter in a medium, heavy saucepan over medium heat. Add the flour and whisk for 1 minute. Gradually whisk in the milk. Bring to a boil over medium-high heat. Reduce the heat to medium and simmer, whisking often, until the sauce thickens slightly, about 5 minutes. Whisk in the nutmeg. Cool slightly. Transfer half of the sauce to a blender. Add the basil and blend until smooth. Return the basil sauce to the sauce in the pan and stir to blend. Season with salt and pepper.

Position a rack in the center of the oven and preheat the oven to 375°F. Lightly butter a 13 × 9 × 2-inch glass baking dish. Spread ¾ cup of the sauce over the prepared baking dish.

Arrange 3 of the lasagna noodles atop the sauce (the noodles will expand as they bake). Pour a third of the squash purée over the noodles and sprinkle with ½ cup of the mozzarella cheese. Drizzle ½ cup of sauce over the mozzarella. Repeat layering the noodles, squash purée, and cheese 2 more times. Top with the remaining 3 noodles. Drizzle with the remaining sauce.

Cover the baking dish tightly with foil and bake for 40 minutes. Uncover the lasagna and sprinkle with the remaining 1 cup of mozzarella and the Parmesan. Continue baking, uncovered, until the sauce bubbles and the top is golden, about 15 minutes longer. Let the lasagna stand for 15 minutes before serving.

note: The no-boil lasagna noodles can be replaced with fresh spinach lasagna sheets. Look for fresh lasagna sheets in the refrigerated section of specialty markets.

insalata di rinforzo

This dish of pickled vegetables is very traditional and we eat it every Christmas Eve as an antipasto. It's supposed to help open and reinforce the stomach for the large meal to come; we just think it's delicious. The assembled platter also makes a lovely centerpiece for the meal.

1 (2-POUND) HEAD OF CAULIFLOWER

3 (16-OUNCE) JARS *GIARDINIERA*, DRAINED

1 (15-OUNCE) CAN BABY CORN, DRAINED AND RINSED

1 (12-OUNCE) JAR ROASTED RED BELL PEPPERS, DRAINED

1 (7.5-OUNCE) JAR BABY PEARL ONIONS, DRAINED

1 (7-OUNCE) JAR GREEN OLIVES, DRAINED

1 (6-OUNCE) JAR PITTED KALAMATA OLIVES, DRAINED

1 (4-OUNCE) JAR CAPERS, DRAINED

⅔ CUP EXTRA-VIRGIN OLIVE OIL

⅓ CUP RED WINE VINEGAR

1 TEASPOON FRESHLY GROUND BLACK PEPPER

Pour 1 inch of water (about 2 cups) into a large, wide pot. Cover and bring the water to a boil over high heat. Add the whole head of cauliflower to the boiling water. Reduce the heat to medium. Cover and steam until a skewer can be inserted easily into the core of the cauliflower, about 8 minutes. Transfer the cauliflower to the center of a large platter. Set aside to cool completely.

Arrange the *giardiniera,* corn, and roasted bell peppers in piles around the cauliflower. Sprinkle the onions, olives, and capers over the vegetables.

In a medium bowl, whisk the oil, vinegar, and black pepper to blend. Drizzle the vinaigrette over the vegetables, and serve. The salad can be prepared ahead. Cover and refrigerate it overnight. Bring the salad to room temperature before serving.

holiday salad

This is a salad my Aunt Raffy makes for every holiday, including Christmas and Thanksgiving. It's a wonderful combination of flavors and a dish that will always remind me of holidays with her.

salad

JUICE OF 1 LEMON

6 MEDIUM BELGIAN ENDIVE, ENDS TRIMMED AND CUT INTO 1-INCH CIRCLES

1 LARGE GREEN APPLE, CORED AND CUT INTO 1-INCH CUBES

1 EAR OF CORN, COOKED AND KERNELS REMOVED, OR 1 CUP DEFROSTED CORN KERNELS

6 OUNCES GRUYÈRE CHEESE, DICED INTO 1-INCH CUBES

1 AVOCADO, DICED INTO 1-INCH CUBES

1 LARGE POMEGRANATE (OPTIONAL)

dressing

⅓ CUP FRESH LEMON JUICE (FROM 2 LEMONS)

½ CUP EXTRA-VIRGIN OLIVE OIL

1 TEASPOON SEA SALT, PLUS MORE TO TASTE

½ TEASPOON FRESHLY GROUND BLACK PEPPER, PLUS MORE TO TASTE

to make the salad

Place half the lemon juice into a large bowl. Add the endive and apples and toss to coat to prevent them from turning brown. Add the corn and cheese, and toss. Drizzle the remaining lemon juice over the avocado cubes and add them to the salad. Cut the pomegranate in half, if using, and carefully remove the seeds. Sprinkle the seeds over the salad.

to make the dressing

Place the lemon juice in a medium bowl. Gradually whisk in the oil and season with 1 teaspoon of the salt and ½ teaspoon of the pepper.

Just before serving, toss the salad with enough dressing to coat. Season the salad to taste with salt and pepper, and serve.

easter pie

Easter is preceded by Lent, a time for fasting. So when Easter Sunday arrives, it is a time to celebrate, splurge, and indulge. You can find this rich, cheesy Easter pie in bakeries all over Italy at that time of year, and every region makes it a little bit differently. This is the Neopolitan version I grew up on.

½ CUP CONFECTIONERS' SUGAR, PLUS MORE FOR SIFTING

4 LARGE EGGS

2 TEASPOONS PURE VANILLA EXTRACT

2 TEASPOONS GRATED ORANGE ZEST

1 (15-OUNCE) CONTAINER WHOLE-MILK RICOTTA CHEESE

1 CUP COOKED SHORT-GRAIN RICE

½ CUP TOASTED PINE NUTS (SEE PAGE 221)

½ CUP (1 STICK) UNSALTED BUTTER, MELTED, PLUS MORE FOR BUTTERING THE PAN

15 SHEETS OF FROZEN PHYLLO DOUGH, THAWED

Blend the confectioners' sugar, eggs, vanilla, and orange zest in a food processor until smooth. Add the ricotta and pulse just until blended. Transfer to a bowl and stir in the rice and pine nuts. Set the ricotta mixture aside.

Preheat the oven to 375°F. Lightly butter a 9-inch-diameter springform pan. Lay 1 sheet of phyllo dough over the bottom and up the sides of the pan, allowing the pastry to hang over the sides. Brush the dough with melted butter. Rotate the pan 90 degrees and lay a second sheet of phyllo dough over the first, allowing the pastry edges to hang over the sides of the pan. Brush with butter. Continue layering the remaining sheets of phyllo dough, turning the pan after each layer and buttering each sheet, to cover the bottom and sides. Spoon the ricotta mixture into the pan. Fold the overhanging phyllo dough over the top of the filling to enclose it completely.

Bake the pie until the phyllo is golden brown and the filling is set, about 1 hour. Transfer the pan to a rack and cool completely. Release the pan sides. Sift more confectioners' sugar over the pie and serve.

pizza rustica

This is not really a pizza; it's another version of Easter Pie (page 199), this time a savory one. Every region in Italy has a different version. This is great to have on hand for lunch or snacks during the holidays when unexpected guests drop by because it can be served warm or at room temperature, and you can reheat individual wedges as needed. To save time, you can make this with store-bought pastry dough.

- 1 (16-OUNCE) BAG FROZEN CHOPPED SPINACH, THAWED AND DRAINED
- 2 TABLESPOONS OLIVE OIL
- 2 TEASPOONS MINCED GARLIC
- SALT AND FRESHLY GROUND BLACK PEPPER
- 1 (15-OUNCE) CONTAINER WHOLE-MILK RICOTTA CHEESE
- ⅓ CUP PLUS 2 TABLESPOONS FRESHLY GRATED PARMESAN CHEESE
- 3 LARGE EGG YOLKS
- 1 RECIPE PASTRY DOUGH (RECIPE FOLLOWS), CHILLED
- ALL-PURPOSE FLOUR, FOR DUSTING
- 3 CUPS SHREDDED MOZZARELLA CHEESE (ABOUT 12 OUNCES)
- 4 OUNCES THINLY SLICED PROSCIUTTO, COARSELY CHOPPED
- 4 OUNCES THINLY SLICED PEPPERONI
- 4 OUNCES THINLY SLICED SALAMI
- 1 (10- TO 12-OUNCE) JAR ROASTED RED BELL PEPPERS, DRAINED
- 1 LARGE EGG, BEATEN

Position the rack on the bottom of the oven, and preheat the oven to 375°F. Squeeze the spinach to drain off as much liquid as possible. Heat the oil in a medium, heavy skillet over medium heat. Add the garlic and sauté until tender, about 1 minute. Add the spinach and sauté until heated through, about 5 minutes. Season to taste with salt and pepper. Transfer the mixture to a large bowl and set aside to cool. Blend the ricotta, ⅓ cup of the Parmesan cheese, and the egg yolks in a food processor, until smooth.

Roll out the larger dough ball on a lightly floured work surface to a 17-inch round. Transfer the dough to a 9-inch springform pan. Sprinkle half of the spinach mixture over the bottom of the dough. Sprinkle ¾ cup of the mozzarella cheese over the spinach. Spread half of the ricotta mixture (about 1 cup) over the mozzarella cheese. Arrange half of each of the

(recipe continues)

prosciutto, pepperoni, and salami atop the ricotta mixture. Sprinkle ¾ cup of the mozzarella over the meats. Arrange half of the roasted peppers in an even layer over the cheese. Sprinkle the remaining spinach mixture over the peppers. Sprinkle ¾ cup of the mozzarella over the spinach. Spread the remaining ricotta mixture over the mozzarella cheese. Arrange the remaining prosciutto, pepperoni, and salami over the ricotta mixture. Sprinkle the remaining ¾ cup of mozzarella cheese over the meats. Arrange the remaining roasted peppers over the cheese.

Roll out the second piece of dough into a 12-inch round. Place the dough over the filling. Pinch the edges of the doughs together to seal. Using scissors, trim the edge of the dough to ½ inch. Fold the dough edges in, creating a decorative rim atop the pizza. Brush some of the egg over the dough. Sprinkle the remaining 2 tablespoons of Parmesan cheese over the top. Bake on the bottom rack until the crust is brown on top and around the sides (cover the top with foil if it begins to brown too quickly, before the sides are brown), about 1 hour.

Let the pizza stand until just warm, about 2 hours. (It can be made 1 day ahead. Cool completely, then cover and refrigerate. Rewarm the pizza in the oven, if desired, or serve it at room temperature.) Release the pan sides and transfer the pizza to a platter. Cut into wedges and serve.

pastry dough

2 CRUSTS

3½ **CUPS ALL-PURPOSE FLOUR**

1 **TEASPOON SALT**

¾ **CUP (1½ STICKS) COLD UNSALTED BUTTER, CUT INTO PIECES**

¼ **CUP COLD SOLID VEGETABLE SHORTENING, CUT INTO PIECES**

3 **LARGE EGGS, BEATEN**

3 **TABLESPOONS ICE WATER, OR MORE AS NEEDED**

Blend the flour and salt in a food processor. Add the butter and shortening and pulse until the mixture resembles a coarse meal. Blend in the eggs. With the machine running, add the water 1 tablespoon at a time until the dough forms. Gather the dough into a ball. Divide the dough into 2 pieces, with 1 piece twice as large as the second piece. Flatten the dough pieces into disks. Wrap in plastic wrap and refrigerate until the dough is firm enough to roll out, about 30 minutes (and up to 1 day).

easter lamb

Lamb in Italy represents spring and renewal, so it's traditionally served at Easter. This is a relatively inexpensive way to make lamb for a large group.

- 2 **TABLESPOONS FENNEL SEEDS**
- 6 **TABLESPOONS (¾ STICK) UNSALTED BUTTER, AT ROOM TEMPERATURE**
- 2 **TABLESPOONS CHOPPED FRESH ROSEMARY**
- 3 **GARLIC CLOVES, MINCED**
  SALT AND FRESHLY GROUND BLACK PEPPER
- 1 **(6-POUND) BONE-IN LEG OF LAMB, TRIMMED OF EXCESS FAT**
- 1¾ **CUPS LOW-SODIUM BEEF BROTH**
- 1½ **CUPS DRY RED WINE**

Using a mallet or heavy rolling pin, crush the fennel seeds in a resealable plastic bag. Transfer the crushed fennel seeds to a small bowl. Add the butter, rosemary, and garlic, and stir to blend. Season the butter with salt and pepper.

Position the rack in the middle of the oven and preheat the oven to 450°F. Place the lamb in a large roasting pan. Pat the lamb dry with paper towels and sprinkle generously with salt and pepper. Rub half of the butter mixture all over the lamb. Refrigerate the remaining butter mixture. Roast the lamb until it is golden brown, about 30 minutes. Decrease the heat to 350°F and continue roasting the lamb until an instant-read meat thermometer registers 135°F when inserted into the thickest part of the meat but not touching the bone, about 45 minutes longer. Transfer the lamb to a platter and tent with foil to keep it warm.

Skim as much fat as possible from the pan juices, then pour the broth and wine into the hot roasting pan. Place the pan over medium-high heat and stir to scrape up the browned bits on the bottom of the pan. Simmer until the juices reduce by half, about 12 minutes. Remove the pan from the heat. Gradually whisk in the remaining cold butter mixture. Season the juices to taste with salt and pepper.

Transfer the juices to a sauceboat. Using a large sharp carving knife, carve the meat into thin slices and arrange on plates. Spoon some of the juices over the meat and serve.

roasted red snapper with parsley vinaigrette

6 SERVINGS

I love cooking fish whole because it guarantees a moist and succulent outcome every time. It looks great, too!

3   RED SNAPPERS (ABOUT 1½ POUNDS EACH), CLEANED AND SCALED BY THE FISHMONGER

3   TABLESPOONS PLUS ¼ CUP EXTRA-VIRGIN OLIVE OIL

½   TEASPOON PAPRIKA

    SALT AND FRESHLY GROUND BLACK PEPPER

1   SWEET ONION (SUCH AS A VIDALIA OR MAUI), CUT INTO PAPER-THIN SLICES

½   CUP FRESH FLAT-LEAF PARSLEY LEAVES

¼   CUP FRESH LEMON JUICE OR RED WINE VINEGAR

2   TEASPOONS DIJON MUSTARD

Preheat the oven to 500°F. Line a large, heavy baking sheet with parchment paper. Place the snapper on the prepared baking sheet. Rub the fish inside and out with 2 tablespoons of the oil, then sprinkle with the paprika, salt, and pepper. Toss the onion in a medium bowl with 1 tablespoon of the oil to coat. Season the onion with salt and pepper. Arrange the onion over the fish. Bake until the snapper is just opaque at the thickest part (test with the tip of a knife) and the onion is tender and beginning to brown, about 20 minutes.

Meanwhile, blend the parsley, lemon juice, and mustard in a blender, until the parsley is finely chopped. Gradually blend in the remaining ¼ cup of oil. Season the vinaigrette with salt and pepper.

Using a metal spatula, transfer the snappers to a platter. Drizzle with the vinaigrette and serve.

linguine with spicy red clam sauce

6 TO 8 SERVINGS

Christmas Eve is the biggest holiday of the year for most Italians. It is the only time of year that my *entire* family (and there are a lot of us) gathers together for a meal at my grandfather's house. The dinner is all about fish. This is *il primo piatto*, the first course of a many-course meal.

2	TABLESPOONS EXTRA-VIRGIN OLIVE OIL
1	ONION, FINELY CHOPPED
6	GARLIC CLOVES, MINCED
1	TABLESPOON DRIED OREGANO
1	TEASPOON CRUSHED DRIED RED PEPPER FLAKES
3	(14½-OUNCE) CANS DICED TOMATOES IN JUICE
2	CUPS BOTTLED CLAM JUICE
1½	CUPS DRY WHITE WINE
4	POUNDS SMALL MANILA CLAMS, SCRUBBED
¼	CUP CHOPPED FRESH FLAT-LEAF PARSLEY
2	TABLESPOONS UNSALTED BUTTER
	SALT
1½	POUNDS DRIED LINGUINE
	FRESHLY GROUND BLACK PEPPER

Heat the oil in a very large pot over medium heat. Add the onion, garlic, oregano, and red pepper flakes. Sauté until the onion is tender, about 10 minutes. Add the tomatoes with their juice, clam juice, and wine. Bring to a boil over high heat. Decrease the heat to medium and simmer uncovered until the liquid reduces by one third, about 30 minutes. Add the clams, cover, and simmer over medium-high heat, stirring occasionally, just until the clams open (discard any clams that do not open), about 8 minutes. Remove the pot from the heat. Using a slotted spoon, transfer the clams to a large bowl and cover to keep them warm. Stir the parsley and butter into the pot.

Meanwhile, bring a large pot of salted water to a boil. Add the linguine and cook, stirring frequently to prevent the pasta from sticking together, until tender but still firm to the bite, about 8 minutes. Drain. Add the linguine to the sauce and toss until the sauce thickens slightly and coats the linguine. Season the pasta generously with salt and black pepper. Transfer the pasta to pasta bowls, top with the clams, and serve.

panettone bread pudding
with amaretto sauce

8 TO 10 SERVINGS

In Italy and in America, a panettone is a traditional hostess gift during the holidays. Though it's great to eat on its own, this may be my favorite way to use up any leftovers. And because all the flavorings are already in the bread, this recipe is simplicity itself.

sauce

½ CUP HEAVY CREAM

½ CUP WHOLE MILK

3 TABLESPOONS SUGAR

¼ CUP AMARETTO LIQUEUR

2 TEASPOONS CORNSTARCH

bread pudding

BUTTER, FOR BAKING DISH

1 (1-POUND) LOAF PANETTONE BREAD, CRUSTS TRIMMED, CUT INTO 1-INCH CUBES

8 LARGE EGGS

1½ CUPS HEAVY CREAM

2½ CUPS WHOLE MILK

1¼ CUPS SUGAR

to make the sauce

Bring the cream, milk, and sugar to a boil in a small, heavy saucepan over medium heat, stirring frequently. In a small bowl, mix the amaretto and cornstarch to blend, then whisk it into the cream mixture. Simmer over medium-low heat, stirring constantly, until the sauce thickens, about 2 minutes. Keep warm or refrigerate up to 3 days and reheat.

to make the bread pudding

Lightly butter a 13 × 9 × 2-inch baking dish. Arrange the bread cubes in the prepared dish. In a large bowl, whisk the eggs, cream, milk, and sugar to blend. Pour the custard over the bread cubes, and press the bread cubes gently to submerge. Let stand for 30 minutes, occasionally pressing the bread cubes into the custard mixture.

Preheat the oven to 350°F. Bake the pudding until it puffs and is set in the center, about 45 minutes. Cool slightly. Spoon the bread pudding into bowls and drizzle with the warm sauce.

family-style
DESSERTS

I have nothing against store-bought desserts, but if you take the trouble to serve a delicious homemade meal, why leave your guests with a memory of dessert from a box? I think there is something truly special about a homemade dessert, and not just because of my sweet tooth! From simple cookies to an elegant Raspberry-Almond Tart, or my just-for-fun Nutella Ravioli and Chocolate Pizza, these Italian desserts will give your dinner an impressive finale with minimal effort.

You'll notice that some of these desserts are not traditionally Italian, but they do feature traditional Italian ingredients like ricotta, mascarpone, and balsamic vinegar, which is just as delicious over berries as it is in a vinaigrette. The thing about Italian desserts is that they taste great and they look great, but they're not very fussy or time-consuming to put together, and they're not especially delicate, either, so they're almost impossible to screw up.

CHOCOLATE ANISE BISCOTTI

CHOCOLATE CHIP COOKIES WITH HAZELNUTS

MOCHA SEMIFREDDO

CHOCOLATE RICOTTA PUDDING
WITH STRAWBERRY SAUCE

RASPBERRY-ALMOND TART

ORANGE SEGMENTS AND BERRIES
WITH BALSAMIC CREAM

NECTARINE AND BLUEBERRY CRISP
WITH AMARETTI COOKIE TOPPING

NUTELLA RAVIOLI

SPICY MOCHA

RASPBERRY TIRAMISU

APRICOT CROSTATA

ESPRESSO BROWNIES

LIMONCELLO CHEESECAKE SQUARES

ZUCCOTTO

CHOCOLATE PIZZA

chocolate anise biscotti

Italians love anise and I love chocolate, so why not combine them in a biscotti? I snack on these crunchy cookies all week long.

2 **CUPS ALL-PURPOSE FLOUR**

1½ **TEASPOONS BAKING POWDER**

¼ **TEASPOON SALT**

¾ **CUP SUGAR**

½ **CUP (1 STICK) UNSALTED BUTTER, AT ROOM TEMPERATURE**

1 **TEASPOON GROUND ANISE SEED**

2 **LARGE EGGS**

1 **CUP SEMISWEET CHOCOLATE CHIPS**

Preheat the oven to 350°F. Line a large, heavy baking sheet with parchment paper. Whisk together the flour, baking powder, and salt in a medium bowl. Using an electric mixer, beat the sugar, butter, and anise seed in a large bowl to blend. Beat in the eggs one at a time. Add the flour mixture and beat just until combined. Stir in the chocolate chips.

Form the dough into a 16-inch-long, 3-inch-wide log. Transfer the log to the prepared baking sheet. Bake until light golden, about 30 minutes. Cool on the baking sheet for 30 minutes.

Place the log on a cutting board. Using a serrated knife, cut the log on the diagonal into ½- to ¾-inch-thick slices. Arrange the biscotti cut side down on the baking sheet. Bake until pale golden, about 15 minutes. Transfer the biscotti to a rack and cool completely. (The biscotti can be prepared 2 days ahead. Store airtight at room temperature.)

Near right, Chocolate Anise Biscotti; far right, Chocolate Chip Cookies with Hazelnuts

chocolate chip cookies with hazelnuts

MAKES 4 DOZEN

If I do say so myself, this is the ultimate chocolate chip cookie. I made five hundred of them for my wedding. I always keep a batch in the freezer for a quick pick-me-up.

½ CUP OLD-FASHIONED (NOT INSTANT) OATS

2¼ CUPS ALL-PURPOSE FLOUR

1 TEASPOON BAKING POWDER

1 TEASPOON BAKING SODA

½ TEASPOON SALT

1 CUP (2 STICKS) UNSALTED BUTTER, AT ROOM TEMPERATURE

1 CUP LIGHT BROWN SUGAR, PACKED

1 CUP GRANULATED SUGAR

2 LARGE EGGS

1 TEASPOON PURE VANILLA EXTRACT

4 OUNCES ENGLISH TOFFEE CANDY (SUCH AS HEATH OR SKOR BAR), FINELY CHOPPED

1 CUP HAZELNUTS, TOASTED, HUSKED, AND CHOPPED (SEE OPPOSITE)

1 (12-OUNCE) BAG SEMISWEET CHOCOLATE CHIPS

Preheat the oven to 325°F. Line 2 large, heavy baking sheets with parchment paper.

Finely chop the oats in a food processor. Transfer the oats to a medium bowl. Mix in the flour, baking powder, baking soda, and salt. Set aside.

Using an electric mixer, beat the butter and sugars in a large bowl until fluffy. Beat in the eggs and vanilla. Add the flour mixture and stir just until blended. Stir in the toffee pieces, hazelnuts, and chocolate chips.

Drop the dough onto the prepared baking sheets by rounded tablespoonful, spacing them 1 inch apart (do not flatten the dough). Bake until the cookies are golden (they will flatten slightly), about 15 minutes. Cool the cookies on the baking sheets for 5 minutes, then transfer them to a cooling rack and cool completely. (The cookies can be prepared 1 day ahead. Store airtight at room temperature.)

HOW TO TOAST NUTS AND SKIN HAZELNUTS

Preheat the oven to 400°F. Place shelled nuts, such as walnuts, almonds, pine nuts, and hazelnuts, on a heavy baking sheet or in a pie tin. Toast the nuts in the oven until they are fragrant and golden brown on the outside and pale golden throughout the inside, stirring occasionally and watching closely to ensure they brown evenly and don't blacken, about 5 to 10 minutes, depending on the size of the nut. Alternatively, preheat a small, heavy skillet over medium-low heat. Place the nuts in the hot skillet and stir them until they become fragrant and golden brown on the outside and pale golden throughout the inside, about 5 minutes.

To remove the dark brown skins on hazelnuts, rub a small handful of cooled toasted hazelnuts at a time briskly between your palms, allowing the skins to fall from your hands and onto a work surface. Don't worry if a few specks of skin remain on the hazelnuts.

mocha semifreddo

Semifreddo means "semifrozen" and this pretty confection slices neatly, just like a cake. Although it requires some time and attention, it's all done ahead and it's a showstopper dessert!

NONSTICK COOKING SPRAY

4 **OUNCES PURCHASED AMARETTI COOKIES (ABOUT 20 SMALL COOKIES)**

3 **TABLESPOONS UNSALTED BUTTER, MELTED**

¾ **CUP SUGAR**

8 **LARGE EGG YOLKS**

⅓ **CUP ESPRESSO**

2 **TABLESPOONS DRY MARSALA**

PINCH OF SALT

1 **CUP HEAVY CREAM**

Spray a 9¼ × 5¼ × 3-inch metal loaf pan lightly with nonstick spray. Line the pan with plastic wrap, allowing the excess to hang over the ends and sides.

Finely grind the cookies in a food processor. Add the melted butter and process until the crumbs are moistened. Press the crumb mixture onto the bottom of the prepared loaf pan. Refrigerate.

Whisk ½ cup of the sugar, the egg yolks, espresso, marsala, and salt in a large metal bowl, to blend. Set the bowl over a saucepan of simmering water (do not allow the bottom of the bowl to touch the water). Whisk the egg mixture until it is thick and creamy and a thermometer inserted into the mixture registers 160ºF, about 5 minutes. Set the custard into another bowl of ice to cool completely.

Using an electric mixer, beat the cream and remaining ¼ cup of sugar in another large bowl until firm peaks form. Using a large rubber spatula, gently fold the whipped cream into the custard. Spoon the mixture onto the prepared crust. Fold the overhanging plastic wrap over the custard and freeze until frozen, at least 8 hours or up to 3 days.

Unfold the plastic wrap. Invert the *semifreddo* onto a platter and peel off the plastic wrap. Cut the *semifreddo* into 1-inch slices and serve.

chocolate ricotta pudding
with strawberry sauce

6 SERVINGS

Ricotta for dessert? I know it sounds a bit odd, but it's used all the time for sweet prepara-tions in Italy, especially in cheesecakes. This is one of my favorite ways to use it. The straw-berry sauce adds a nice, tart accent that is a little lighter than a raspberry purée would be. Try to find really red, ripe berries for the most flavorful sauce.

sauce

2	CUPS FRESH STRAWBERRIES
2	TABLESPOONS SUGAR

pudding

	BUTTER, FOR GREASING THE CUPS
6	OUNCES BITTERSWEET CHOCOLATE (NOT UNSWEETENED), CHOPPED
1½	POUNDS FRESH WHOLE-MILK RICOTTA CHEESE, DRAINED IN A FINE-MESH STRAINER FOR 2 HOURS TO REMOVE EXCESS LIQUID
¼	CUP PLUS ⅓ CUP SUGAR
3	LARGE EGGS, SEPARATED
1	TEASPOON ORANGE ZEST
½	TEASPOON PURE ALMOND EXTRACT
¼	TEASPOON GROUND CINNAMON
⅛	TEASPOON SALT
¼	TEASPOON CREAM OF TARTAR

to make the sauce

Blend the strawberries and sugar in a food processor until smooth. Strain the purée through a fine-mesh strainer. Cover and refrigerate. (Can be made 8 hours ahead. Keep refrigerated.)

to make the pudding

Preheat the oven to 325°F. Lightly butter six 6-ounce custard cups. Arrange the cups in a large roasting pan. Melt the chocolate in a medium bowl set over a saucepan of simmering water. Stir until smooth, then set the melted chocolate aside. Blend the ricotta, ¼ cup of the sugar, the egg yolks, orange zest, almond extract, cinnamon, and salt in a food processor until very smooth. Blend in the melted chocolate. Transfer the ricotta mixture to a large bowl.

Using an electric mixer with the whisk attachment, beat the egg whites in another large bowl with the cream of tartar until soft peaks form. Gradually beat in the remaining ⅓ cup of sugar. Continue beating until semifirm peaks form. Carefully fold the egg whites into the ricotta mixture.

Spoon the mixture into the prepared cups. Fill the pan with enough hot water to come halfway up the sides of the custard cups. Bake until the puddings puff slightly but the centers are still creamy, about 25 minutes (the pudding will become thick when cold). Remove the custard cups from the water bath. Cool slightly. Cover and refrigerate until cold, about 3 hours.

Run a knife around the sides of the puddings to loosen. Invert the puddings onto plates. Drizzle the strawberry sauce around the puddings and serve.

raspberry-almond tart

Store-bought puff pastry has many uses but few that beat this one—this happens to be the fastest and prettiest tart you'll ever make. You can use any fruit that's in season, including orange segments, berries, plums, bananas, or even grapes. Blueberries make a good substitute for the raspberries, and sliced peaches or nectarines are delicious as well. As you can see, this is an extremely versatile recipe; once you've made it a few times, it will become an easy standby.

1 SHEET OF FROZEN PUFF PASTRY (FROM A 17¼-OUNCE PACKAGE), THAWED

ALL-PURPOSE FLOUR, FOR DUSTING

1 LARGE EGG, LIGHTLY BEATEN

¾ CUP HEAVY CREAM

¼ CUP CONFECTIONERS' SUGAR

2 TABLESPOONS AMARETTO LIQUEUR

¼ CUP TOASTED SLICED ALMONDS, COARSELY CRUMBLED (SEE PAGE 221)

2 (6-OUNCE) BASKETS OF FRESH RASPBERRIES

UNSWEETENED COCOA POWDER, FOR DUSTING

Preheat the oven to 400°F. Cut a ¾-inch-wide strip off each edge of the pastry and reserve.

Roll out the pastry sheet on a lightly floured work surface to a 10-inch square. Brush the edges of the square with the egg. Arrange the 4 pastry strips atop the edges of the pastry square, overlapping on the corners and forming a raised border. If necessary, stretch the strips to cover each edge or trim any overhanging strips. Brush the border with the egg. Pierce the center of the pastry all over with a fork. Bake until the pastry is golden brown, about 20 minutes. Carefully slide it onto a rack and cool completely.

Using an electric mixer, beat the cream, sugar, and liqueur in a large bowl until firm peaks form. Fold in the nuts. Spoon the cream mixture into the prepared pastry crust. Arrange the berries over the cream. Sift the cocoa powder over the tart and serve.

orange segments and berries
with balsamic cream

This recipe is all about the balsamic cream. The vinegar becomes thick and syrupy and very sweet when it's reduced. Use it like you would a chocolate sauce; it's fabulous over ice cream or frozen yogurt. I tend to make this a lot in the winter months when citrus fruits are the best offerings at the produce stand.

- 4 **NAVEL ORANGES**
- ¾ **CUP INEXPENSIVE BALSAMIC VINEGAR**
- ⅓ **CUP CRÈME FRAÎCHE**
- 1 **TEASPOON SUGAR**
- 12 **OUNCES FRESH STRAWBERRIES, QUARTERED**

With a very sharp knife, cut the peel and white pith from the oranges. Cut between the membranes to release the segments.

In a small, heavy saucepan over medium-high heat, whisk the vinegar, crème fraîche, and sugar until the mixture thickens and resembles chocolate sauce, about 8 minutes.

Arrange the orange segments and strawberries decoratively on dessert plates. Drizzle the warm balsamic sauce over the fruit and serve. Alternatively, the balsamic sauce can be served at room temperature and spooned over the fruit.

nectarine and blueberry crisp with amaretti cookie topping

I like to make this in the summer when I have lots of ripe nectarines and the blueberries are at their best. My favorite part is the crust, which is light, sweet, and crunchy, and tastes just incredible with the mascarpone, an Italian stand-in for the more expected whipped cream or vanilla ice cream. Make the filling with any of your favorite fruits.

topping

1 CUP ALL-PURPOSE FLOUR

⅓ CUP LIGHT BROWN SUGAR, FIRMLY PACKED

⅓ CUP GRANULATED SUGAR

½ CUP (1 STICK) UNSALTED BUTTER, CUT INTO ½-INCH PIECES

1 CUP CRUSHED AMARETTI COOKIES, COARSELY CRUSHED

¾ CUP SLICED ALMONDS

filling

BUTTER, FOR BAKING DISH

2 TABLESPOONS GRANULATED SUGAR

2 TABLESPOONS ALL-PURPOSE FLOUR

3 POUNDS NECTARINES, PITTED AND CUT INTO WEDGES

8 OUNCES BLUEBERRIES

3 TABLESPOONS AMARETTO LIQUEUR

½ CUP MASCARPONE CHEESE

to make the topping

Stir the flour and sugars in a medium bowl to blend. Add the butter and rub between your fingertips until moist clumps form. Mix in the amaretti crumbs and almonds.

to make the filling

Preheat the oven to 350°F. Butter a 13 × 9 × 2-inch glass baking dish. Stir the sugar and flour in a large bowl. Add the nectarines and blueberries, and toss to combine. Stir in the liqueur.

Spoon the fruit mixture into the prepared dish. Sprinkle the cookie topping over. Bake until the nectarines are tender and the topping is golden and crisp, about 45 minutes. Cool for at least 10 minutes. Spoon the warm crisp into bowls. Top each with a dollop of mascarpone cheese and serve.

nutella ravioli

Ravioli for dessert! Need I say more?

16 WONTON WRAPPERS

1 LARGE EGG, LIGHTLY BEATEN

1 CUP CHOCOLATE-HAZELNUT SPREAD (SUCH AS NUTELLA)

VEGETABLE OIL, FOR FRYING

16 FRESH MINT LEAVES

NONSTICK COOKING SPRAY

GRANULATED SUGAR, FOR DREDGING

CONFECTIONERS' SUGAR, FOR DUSTING

Line a baking sheet with plastic wrap. Place 1 wonton wrapper on a work surface. Brush the edges of the wrapper lightly with egg. Spoon 1 tablespoon of chocolate-hazelnut spread into the center of the wrapper. Fold the wrapper diagonally over the filling and press the edges of the wrapper to seal. Place the ravioli on the prepared baking sheet. Repeat with the remaining wonton wrappers and chocolate-hazelnut spread.

Preheat the oven to 200° F. Add enough oil to a large, heavy frying pan to reach a depth of 2 inches. Heat the oil over medium heat to 350ºF. Working in 3 batches, carefully add the ravioli to the hot oil and cook until they are golden brown, about 45 seconds per side. Using a slotted spoon, transfer the ravioli to a plate lined with paper towels to drain. Then, transfer the cooked ravioli to another baking sheet, and keep them warm in the oven while frying the remaining ravioli. (The fried ravioli can be prepared 1 day ahead. Cool them completely, then cover and refrigerate. Before serving, place them on a baking sheet and rewarm in a 375ºF oven just until they are heated through, about 7 minutes.)

Spray the top side of the mint leaves very lightly with nonstick cooking spray. Working with 1 leaf at a time, dredge the coated side of the leaves in granulated sugar to coat lightly.

Arrange 2 fried ravioli on each plate. Dust the ravioli with confectioners' sugar. Garnish with the sugared mint leaves and serve.

spicy mocha

Who doesn't love hot chocolate on a cold wintery day? This is my Italian twist! I especially love to serve this when I'm off on a ski vacation.

- 4½ CUPS WHOLE MILK
- 4 SMALL DRIED RED CHILES (SUCH AS CHILES DE ARBOL)
- 3 CINNAMON STICKS, BROKEN IN HALF
- 3 CUPS BREWED ESPRESSO
- 1½ CUPS SUGAR
- 1¼ CUPS UNSWEETENED COCOA POWDER
- ½ CUP CONFECTIONERS' SUGAR
- 1 CUP HEAVY CREAM

Combine the milk, chiles, and cinnamon sticks in a large, heavy saucepan. Bring to a simmer over high heat. Remove from the heat. Cover and steep for 15 minutes. Whisk in the espresso, sugar, and 1 cup of the cocoa powder. Bring the hot chocolate to a simmer, whisking often. Discard the chiles and cinnamon sticks.

Meanwhile, whisk the confectioners' sugar and remaining ¼ cup of cocoa powder in a large bowl to blend. Add the cream and whisk until the mixture is thick.

Ladle the hot chocolate into 8 mugs. Spoon the chocolate whipped cream atop and serve immediately.

raspberry tiramisù

There's nothing wrong with the classic tiramisù of ladyfingers soaked in espresso topped with marsala and mascarpone cream, but my version is a lot lighter and more beautiful. The great thing about this dessert is that you actually *have* to prepare it ahead of time. The longer it sits, the better it tastes.

- 1 **CUP SEEDLESS RASPBERRY JAM**
- 6 **TABLESPOONS GRAND MARNIER**
- 1 **POUND MASCARPONE CHEESE, AT ROOM TEMPERATURE**
- 1 **CUP HEAVY CREAM**
- ¼ **CUP GRANULATED SUGAR**
- 1 **TEASPOON PURE VANILLA EXTRACT**
- 48 **SOFT LADYFINGERS (2 3-OUNCE PACKAGES) OR 40 DRY ITALIAN LADYFINGERS (2 PACKAGES)**
- 3 **BASKETS FRESH RASPBERRIES (½ DRY PINT, ABOUT 3¾ CUPS TOTAL)**
  CONFECTIONERS' SUGAR, FOR DUSTING

Stir together the jam and 4 tablespoons of the Grand Marnier in a small bowl to blend.

Stir together the mascarpone and remaining 2 tablespoons of Grand Marnier in a large bowl to blend. Using an electric mixer, beat the cream, granulated sugar, and vanilla in another large bowl until soft peaks form. Using a large rubber spatula, stir a fourth of the whipped cream into the mascarpone mixture to lighten. Fold the remaining whipped cream into the mascarpone mixture.

Line the bottom of a 13 × 9 × 2-inch glass baking dish or other decorative serving dish with a third of the ladyfingers. Spread a third of the jam mixture over the ladyfingers. Spread a third of the mascarpone mixture over the jam mixture, then cover with a third of the fresh raspberries. Repeat layering with the remaining ladyfingers, jam mixture, mascarpone mixture, and raspberries. Cover and refrigerate at least 3 hours or overnight.

Dust the confectioners' sugar over the top and serve.

apricot crostata

In Italy this dessert is more of a breakfast item or an afternoon snack to serve with coffee. I think it's perfect anytime and it's a good pantry dessert to have up your sleeve when unexpected guests drop by—just use any kind of jam or preserves you happen to have on hand; I also love raspberry.

1½ CUPS ALL-PURPOSE FLOUR

2 TABLESPOONS SUGAR

GRATED ZEST OF 1 LEMON

¼ TEASPOON SALT

10 TABLESPOONS (1¼ STICKS) UNSALTED BUTTER, CHILLED AND CUT INTO ½-INCH PIECES

3 TABLESPOONS ICE WATER

¾ CUP APRICOT PRESERVES

1 TABLESPOON TOASTED SLICED ALMONDS (SEE PAGE 221)

CONFECTIONERS' SUGAR, FOR DUSTING

Combine the flour, sugar, lemon zest, and salt in a food processor and whir to blend. Add the butter and pulse until the mixture resembles a coarse meal. Add the ice water bit by bit, pulsing until moist clumps form. Gather the dough into a ball; flatten it into a disk. Wrap the dough in plastic and refrigerate until firm, about 1 hour.

Position the rack in the center of the oven and preheat the oven to 400°F. Roll out the dough on a large sheet of parchment paper to an 11-inch round. Transfer the dough on the parchment paper to a large, heavy baking sheet. Spread the preserves over the dough, leaving a 2-inch border. Fold the dough border over the filling to form an 8-inch round, pleating the crust loosely and pinching to seal any cracks in the dough.

Bake the crostata until the crust is golden, about 40 minutes. Put the baking sheet on a rack to cool for 10 minutes, then slide a metal spatula under the crust to free the crostata from the parchment. Cool the crostata to lukewarm. Sprinkle with the almonds and dust with the confectioners' sugar. Transfer the crostata to a platter and serve.

espresso brownies

In my opinion, these are the quintessential brownies—they're smooth and dense and ooze chocolate from all the chocolate chips. These brownies satisfy both my chocolate *and* coffee cravings; whenever I make them, I freeze them in small batches so that I'm not tempted to eat them all in one sitting.

⅓ **CUP PLUS 2 TABLESPOONS WATER**

⅓ **CUP VEGETABLE OIL**

2 **LARGE EGGS**

2 **TABLESPOONS PLUS 2 TEASPOONS ESPRESSO POWDER**

1 **19.8-OUNCE BOX BROWNIE MIX (SUCH AS DUNCAN HINES)**

¾ **CUP SEMISWEET CHOCOLATE CHIPS**

1 **TEASPOON VANILLA EXTRACT**

1½ **CUPS CONFECTIONERS' SUGAR**

1 **TABLESPOON UNSALTED BUTTER, AT ROOM TEMPERATURE**

Preheat the oven to 350°F. Grease a 9 × 9-inch baking pan.

Whisk together ⅓ cup of the water, the oil, eggs, and 2 tablespoons of the espresso powder in a large bowl. Add the brownie mix and stir until well blended. Stir in the chocolate chips. Transfer the batter to the prepared baking pan. Bake until a toothpick inserted into the center of the brownies comes out with a few moist crumbs attached, about 35 minutes. Transfer the pan to a wire rack to cool completely.

When the brownies are cool, dissolve the remaining 2 teaspoons of espresso powder in the remaining 2 tablespoons of water in a medium bowl. Whisk in the vanilla. Add the confectioners' sugar and butter and whisk until smooth. With the brownies still in the pan, pour the glaze over the brownies. Refrigerate until the glaze is set. Cut into bite-size pieces, arrange the brownies on a platter, and serve.

limoncello cheesecake squares

12 TO 16 SERVINGS

Refreshing, light, and decadent, these ethereal squares are a cross between mini cheese-cakes and everyone's favorite lemon bars. The flavors remind me of summers in Capri, where they make the best *limoncello.*

NONSTICK COOKING SPRAY

8 **OUNCES PURCHASED BISCOTTI**

6 **TABLESPOONS (¾ STICK) UNSALTED BUTTER, MELTED**

3 **TABLESPOONS GRATED LEMON ZEST**

1 **(12-OUNCE) CONTAINER FRESH WHOLE-MILK RICOTTA CHEESE, DRAINED**

2 **(8-OUNCE) PACKAGES CREAM CHEESE, AT ROOM TEMPERATURE**

1¼ **CUPS SUGAR**

½ **CUP *LIMONCELLO* (SEE NOTE)**

2 **TEASPOONS PURE VANILLA EXTRACT**

4 **LARGE EGGS**

Preheat the oven to 350°F. Spray the bottom of a 9 × 9 × 2-inch baking pan with nonstick cooking spray. Break the biscotti into pieces and grind them to fine crumbs in a food processor. Add the melted butter and 1 tablespoon of the lemon zest, and process until the crumbs are moistened. Press the crumb mixture over just the bottom (not the sides) of the prepared pan. Bake until the crust is golden, about 15 minutes. Transfer the pan to a cooling rack and cool the crust completely.

Clean out the food processor bowl and blend the ricotta until smooth. Add the cream cheese and sugar, and blend well, stopping the machine occasionally and scraping down the sides. Blend in the *limoncello,* vanilla, and the remaining 2 tablespoons of lemon zest. Add the eggs and pulse just until blended.

Pour the cheese mixture over the crust in the pan. Place the baking pan in a large roasting pan. Pour enough hot water into the roasting pan to come halfway up the sides of the smaller pan. Bake until the cheesecake is golden but the center of the cake moves slightly when the pan is gently shaken, about 1 hour (the cheesecake will firm up as it cools).

Transfer the pan to a rack; cool for 1 hour. Refrigerate until the cheesecake is cold, at least 8 hours and up to 2 days. Cut the cake into squares and serve.

note You can use either the Limoncello recipe on page 188 or purchased *limoncello. Limoncello* liqueur can be found at most liquor stores and some specialty markets.

zuccotto

Desserts don't get much showier than this. The shape is meant to recall the dome-shaped ceiling of the cathedrals in Italy. I love the way this dessert looks when it's inverted, and the taste is pure decadence. If you use a purchased pound cake, which I recommend, it's not at all hard to make.

NONSTICK COOKING SPRAY

1 **(12-OUNCE) LOAF OF POUND CAKE**

⅓ **CUP BRANDY**

6 **OUNCES BITTERSWEET CHOCOLATE, CHOPPED**

2 **CUPS CHILLED HEAVY CREAM**

¼ **CUP CONFECTIONERS' SUGAR**

½ **TEASPOON PURE ALMOND EXTRACT**

½ **CUP SLICED ALMONDS, TOASTED AND COARSELY CRUMBLED (SEE PAGE 221)**

UNSWEETENED COCOA POWDER, FOR DUSTING

Spray a 1½-quart bowl with nonstick spray. Line the bowl with plastic wrap. Cut the pound cake crosswise into ⅓-inch-thick slices. Cut each slice diagonally in half, forming two triangles. Line the bottom and sides of the prepared bowl with the cake triangles. Brush some of the brandy over the cake triangles lining the bowl. Reserve the extra triangles.

Stir the chocolate in a large metal bowl set over a saucepan of simmering water until it melts. Set it aside and let the chocolate cool to room temperature. Using an electric mixer, beat 1 cup of the cream in another large bowl until it is thick and fluffy. Fold one fourth of the whipped cream into the chocolate. Then fold half of the remaining whipped cream into the chocolate mixture, and finally fold in the remaining whipped cream. Spread the chocolate cream over the cake, covering completely and creating a well in the center. Cover and refrigerate while you make the second filling.

Using an electric mixer with clean beaters, in a clean large bowl, beat the remaining 1 cup of cream, the confectioners' sugar, and almond extract until firm peaks form. Fold in the nuts. Spoon the cream mixture into the center well of the filling.

Brush the remaining cake slices on one side with brandy and arrange them, brandy side down, over the cake, covering the filling completely and trimming to fit if necessary. Cover the cake with plastic wrap and refrigerate at least 3 hours and up to 1 day.

Invert the cake onto a platter. Remove the bowl and the plastic wrap. Dust with cocoa powder and serve.

chocolate pizza

This is a witty variation on the classic and it's especially fun to make with kids!

- 1 **POUND HOMEMADE OR PURCHASED PIZZA DOUGH**
- 2 **TEASPOONS UNSALTED BUTTER, MELTED**
- ¼ **CUP CHOCOLATE-HAZELNUT SPREAD (SUCH AS NUTELLA)**
- ½ **CUP SEMISWEET CHOCOLATE CHIPS**
- 2 **TABLESPOONS MILK CHOCOLATE CHIPS**
- 2 **TABLESPOONS WHITE CHOCOLATE CHIPS**
- 2 **TABLESPOONS CHOPPED TOASTED HAZELNUTS**

Position the oven rack on the bottom of the oven and preheat to 450°F. Line a large, heavy baking sheet with parchment paper. Roll out the dough to a 9-inch-diameter round and transfer to the prepared baking sheet.

Using your fingertips, make indentations all over the dough. Brush the dough with the melted butter, then bake until the crust is crisp and pale golden brown, about 20 minutes. Immediately spread a thin layer of the chocolate-hazelnut spread over the crust, then sprinkle with the chocolate chips.

Return to the oven and bake just until the chips begin to melt, about 1 minute. Sprinkle the hazelnuts over the pizza, cut into wedges, and serve.

note This basic recipe can be altered to taste in a plethora of ways. Consider other ingredients, either as substitutions or additions, such as shaved coconut, pistachios, dried fruit, or marshmallows. You could even use raspberry jam instead of the chocolate-hazelnut spread.

menus for family dinners

christmas menu
Insalata di Rinforzo
Linguine with Spicy Red Clam Sauce
Roasted Red Snapper with Parsley Vinaigrette
Sautéed Green Beans with Tomatoes and Basil
Panettone Bread Pudding with Amaretto Sauce
Rosé Wine with Fresh Sage and Lemon

thanksgiving menu
Limoncello Spritzers
Turkey with Herbes de Provence and Citrus
Ciabatta Stuffing with Chestnuts and Pancetta
Butternut Squash Lasagna
Holiday Salad
Nectarine and Blueberry Crisp with Amaretti Cookie Topping

easter menu
Bellini Bar
Easter Lamb
Baked Mashed Potatoes with Parmesan Cheese and Bread Crumbs
Broccoli Florets with Meyer Lemon Olive Oil
Pizza Rustica
Easter Pie

cold-weather get-together
Tomato Soup with Pancetta
Pot Roast with Porcini Mushrooms (Straccoto)
Herbed Cheese Polenta
Braised Swiss Chard
Espresso Brownies
Spicy Mocha

backyard barbecue
Swordfish Spiedini

Stuffed Artichokes

Grilled Lettuces

Roasted Eggplant and Tomatoes

Apricot Crostata

celebratory dinner
Limoncello Spritzers

Pizzettes with Gorgonzola, Tomato, and Basil

Salami Crisps with Sour Cream and Basil

Little Thimbles Sciue' Sciue'

Grilled Chicken with Basil Dressing

Italian Caesar Salad

Raspberry Tiramisù

kid-friendly dinner
Sun-Dried Tomato and Mozzarella Kebabs

Broccoli Florets with Meyer Lemon Olive Oil

Parmesan-Crusted Pork Chops

Chocolate Chip Cookies with Hazelnuts

elegant dinner
Red Wine Risotto with Peas

Broiled Salmon with Garlic, Mustard, and Herbs

Sautéed Green Beans with Tomatoes and Basil

Mocha Semifreddo

index